Hitler's Air Defences

Hitler's Air Defences

Stephen Wynn

Pen & Sword
MILITARY
AN IMPRINT OF PEN & SWORD BOOKS LTD.
YORKSHIRE – PHILADELPHIA

First published in Great Britain in 2021 by
Pen & Sword Military
An imprint of
Pen & Sword Books Ltd
Yorkshire - Philadelphia

ISBN 978 1 52674 026 7

Printed and bound in England
By CPI Group (UK) Ltd., Croydon, CR0 4YY

Pen & Sword Books Ltd. incorporates the Imprints of Pen & Sword
Archaeology, Atlas, Aviation, Battleground, Discovery, Family History,
History, Maritime, Military, Naval, Politics, Railways, Select, Transport,
True Crime, Fiction, Frontline Books, Leo Cooper, Praetorian Press,
Seaforth Publishing, Wharncliffe and White Owl.

For a complete list of Pen & Sword titles please contact

PEN & SWORD BOOKS LIMITED
47 Church Street, Barnsley, South Yorkshire, S70 2AS, England
E-mail: enquiries@pen-and-sword.co.uk
Website: www.pen-and-sword.co.uk

or

PEN AND SWORD BOOKS
1950 Lawrence Rd, Havertown, PA 19083, USA
E-mail: uspen-and-sword@casematepublishers.com
Website: www.penandswordbooks.com

Contents

Introduction   vi

Chapter 1   The Flak Corps   1

Chapter 2   The Butt Report   14

Chapter 3   German Successes   24

Chapter 4   United States Intelligence Bulletin   41

Chapter 5   Raid on Regensburg and Schweinfurt –
                17 August 1943   58

Chapter 6   Combined Bomber Offensive   72

Chapter 7   German Searchlight Units   77

Chapter 8   German Barrage Balloons   84

Chapter 9   Chaff and Electronic Counter Measures   89

Chapter 10 Newspaper Articles   109

Chapter 11 Air Raids on German Cities   144

Chapter 12 Press Reports of German Air Defences   155

Chapter 13 German Aircraft Production   171

Chapter 14 The Bombing of Dresden   173

Chapter 15 The 88mm Artillery Gun   179

In Closing   189

About the Author   191

Sources   193

Index   194

Introduction

To provide a fair and unbiased picture of Hitler's air defences and their effectiveness during the Second World War, consideration must be given to what they had to contend with, which differed significantly throughout the course of the war. In the early months there was no real need for anything too sophisticated in the way of air defences because Germany wasn't fighting the war on her own soil. Immediately after the Luftwaffe's Blitzkrieg attacks on neighbouring Poland – between September 1939 and April 1940 – nothing really happened in a fighting sense.

The Second World War began because of the Third Reich's invasion of Poland, which directly led to both France and Great Britain declaring war. But then there was nothing. Rather than all three nations 'having at each other' straight away, it was some seven months before any significant land or air action took place between the warring factions. History has recorded this period of time as the 'Phoney War'. It is a phrase that was supposedly coined by the American senator, William Edgar Borah, who was anti-war and also against American resources being used to support any Western democracies in the war, particularly France and Great Britain.

In Germany the 'Phoney War' was referred to as the 'Sitzkrieg' which translates as 'The Sitting War'. It would have been an ideal time for either Britain or France to have attacked Germany as her defences, particularly her air defences, were basically non-existent, but for some inexplicable reason no such attack was forthcoming.

As the war started in earnest, it became apparent that the initial German approach was somewhat tentative. When Nazi Germany invaded Poland on 1 September 1939, part of their invasion plan involved the Luftwaffe and the shock effect of Ju-87 *Stuka* dive bomber attacks, many of which were indiscriminate in their targets. In total Germany deployed more than 1,200 aircraft in her invasion of Poland.

Compare that to Germany's first attack on mainland Britain, which came in the shape of a Luftwaffe raid on the Firth of Forth in Scotland on 16 October 1939, where their pilots were under strict orders to be selective in what they attacked so as to minimise the chance of inflicting civilian casualties. On 18 December 1939, RAF Bomber Command sent its Wellington bombers to attack targets in the Heligoland Bight, a bay which is part of the southern part of the German Bight at the mouth of the River Elbe. The bomber crews were under strict instructions not to attack civilian living quarters, merchant shipping or any land-based sites. It was as if by only attacking military targets and avoiding civilian casualties, each side was not only holding back from all-out war, but both Britain and Germany were giving themselves room to manoeuvre in the hope that they could come to some form of agreement before they reached a point of no return.

By May 1940 it was abundantly clear that there would be no peace between Britain and Germany. On its first night raid against mainland Germany over the Ruhr industrial area, the RAF deployed 99 bomber aircraft, 98 of which made it back to their bases in England. This revealed how ineffective German air defences were at that time; whether that ineffectiveness was down to there not being enough air defence units, or the poor quality of those who manned them is unclear. It is likely to have been the former.

The effectiveness of German anti-aircraft batteries increased as the number of Royal Air Force and United States Air Force air attacks on mainland Germany multiplied. Nowhere was this displayed with better effect than the Allied raid on Schweinfurt on 14 October 1943, which was carried out by American Flying Fortresses and Liberators of the USAAF. The efficiency that day of the German anti-aircraft units was devastating.

As the war continued different factors became involved in the effectiveness of German air defences. Since the Americans had entered the war on the side of the Allies, Germany was being attacked day and night. Daytime attacks made it easier for the German anti-aircraft units, whilst night-time attacks handed the advantage back to the attacking Allied aircraft. Bombing raids that struck targets deep into Germany meant aircraft being in the air longer, providing more opportunity for the anti-aircraft units to shoot them down.

By the end of 1943, the air supremacy that the Allies had been enjoying over Germany had been lost. Hundreds of thousands of civilians and soldiers had been utilised to form a stronger defensive network of early detection systems, coupled with a web of heavy anti-aircraft batteries. As the war continued, so did the advancements in aircraft tactics, navigation systems, and the munitions used, whilst at the same time Germany was finding it harder to produce and replace much needed military hardware and the personnel required to defend the nation.

Hitler's air defences had been effective to a point in defending Germany, especially in the early part of the war. But with America's intervention from 7 December 1941, Germany ended up having to endure air attacks 24 hours a day. From 30 May 1942, she also had to endure the staggering power of the 'Thousand-bomber raids'. No matter how many anti-aircraft units Germany could deploy, and how accurate their gunners were, they were never going to be effective enough to be able to defend their homeland properly. Committed Nazi or proud German, no level of commitment could have held at bay what the RAF and the USAAF were collectively capable of delivering.

In addition, the anti-aircraft batteries and Flak Corps, which had been developed and manufactured by Nazi Germany, were also used in many of the countries which she occupied during the war. Added to this is the fact that in the years leading up to the outbreak of the Second World War, beginning from the Nazi's rise to power in 1933, war had always been part of their agenda, it was a case of when rather than if. The only way war would have been avoided was if Britain had continued to acquiesce to Germany's military actions and demands as she began asserting her military strength.

The Second World War did not just happen, it was planned by Nazi Germany, because September 1939 was the time when Hitler believed that they were not only ready to go to war, but capable of winning it. In all of the planning for war, Hitler appears to have made a basic and fundamental mistake by taking the final outcome of the war as a forgone conclusion. In his planning, little or no consideration was given to the possibility that there would be a time where Germany would have to defend herself from air attack from her enemies. Because of this glaring oversight the equipment that was needed to defend Germany wasn't in place at the beginning of the war, certainly not in the amounts that were needed.

Hitler had only planned for an offensive war and had given little consideration to Germany's own defences. This was a massive mistake. The other mistake was in not targeting Allied air production which had allowed them to build large numbers of aircraft, both bombers and fighters, which eventually led to the 'Thousand-bomber raids' on German cities and factories that had helped build and maintain the German war effort. The first of these raids, code named Operation Millennium, took place on the night of 30/31 May 1942, when the city of Cologne was bombed. The purpose of the raid was an attempt by the Allies to make Germany surrender, or at least cause severe damage to German morale, both within the military and the civilian population.

What Hitler could not have known was that the attack on Cologne was also a major turning point in the war for Britain. Prior to this, and mainly throughout 1941, Bomber Command's reputation, and that of the man in charge of it, Sir Arthur Travers Harris, were at an all-time low. The poor performance of its aircraft, especially its bombing accuracy, had led to calls for Harris's unit to be split up and its aircraft and men deployed to other theatres of war. If Harris 'got it right' with the raid on Cologne, not only was he likely to keep his unit, but also convince the War Cabinet that Bomber Command was worth enlarging in size. But before any of this could be achieved, Harris first needed to find sufficient aircraft for the proposed raid. He ended up with 1,160 aircraft, of which 113 were used to attack airfields where the Luftwaffe's night fighters operated.

The belief was that with so many aircraft in the skies over Cologne, it would reduce the time of the overall raid, which it did, from four hours to ninety minutes. This was an advantage in two ways for Bomber Command, because it meant that it was more difficult for Germany's anti-aircraft batteries to be able to focus on specific targets, and with the raid time reduced Allied bombers spent less time in the air.

The raid, which saw more than twice the number of British bombers dispatched than ever before, dropped 1,455 tons of bombs, two thirds of them incendiaries. The destruction and devastation caused by the subsequent fires and explosions was immense. Some 40,000 homes and buildings were damaged or destroyed, and more than 20,000 of the city's population were killed. Out of all the properties that were damaged, only one had a military significance – the barracks of the men who served on the anti-aircraft units.

Of the 43 bombers that were lost on the raid, only 16 were brought down by the German defensive flak units, which in real terms was not a very high success rate, but then having to deal with so many enemy aircraft in the one raid, their job was certainly not an easy one.

The original target for the raid was Germany's second largest city, Hamburg. One of the main attractions for the raid taking place there was that it was a port city, where on average somewhere in the region of 100 submarines were built each year. But because of inclement weather throughout Germany for the three days leading up to the raid, it was decided to attack Cologne instead, with the decision only being taken as late as lunchtime on the day of the raid.

CHAPTER 1

The Flak Corps

The responsibility for German air defence, along with important areas of occupied countries, came under the control of the chief of the Luftwaffe. Each unit had anti-aircraft artillery pieces, searchlights and barrage balloons. Each of these units, or *Flakgruppen*, as they were called, had good liaison and communications with their local air raid warning centre, as well as the fighter interceptor units. Each *Flakgruppen* did not necessarily have the same manpower or equipment; these two elements were dependent on the role that they were expected to play in the overall defence strategy.

Most heavy Flak batteries consisted of four to six heavy guns, which more often than not were 88mm artillery pieces. They were usually also equipped with at least two light 20mm guns for protecting the battery from an infantry attack. Light Flak batteries had a different configuration of weapons, usually around a dozen 37mm or 20mm guns. Depending on the purpose of the unit and what it was actually in place to protect, would determine exactly where it would be located. Some would be at ground level in a fixed position, whilst others would be on top of the buildings or factories that they were in place to protect.

The Germans had put a lot of thought into their deployment of anti-aircraft batteries. There certainly wasn't any rigidity involved, in fact quite the opposite. The main tactic was flexibility. Part of this included having some of their artillery pieces on flat railway carriages, so that they could be moved to where they were needed in double quick time. The other aspect of their tactics which displayed a lot of intelligence was to move their anti-aircraft batteries from one position to another, whilst still being in a position to protect the location they were guarding. Part of the reason behind this was undoubtedly for self-preservation, as the Germans would have been well aware that reconnaissance photographs were taken of their locations during air raids, providing British and American planners with valuable information about how and where the German defences were. This allowed them to be targeted, as well providing the planners with information on potentially easy routes their aircraft could take to their target on the next raid. If the defended locations were of significance, they would be repeatedly attacked until they were put out of action.

The thought process did not end there. When it came to opening fire on RAF and USAAF bombers, the methods used would differ depending on whether it was a daytime or night-time raid. Their tactics changed all the time. Sometimes they would wait until an Allied bomber was caught in a searchlight beam before opening fire. Sometimes, once the anti-aircraft units could hear the sound of the bombers' engines they would open fire in the general direction of where the noise was coming from. Sometimes, just one artillery piece would open fire, whilst on other occasions the entire battery would open up.

The Flak corps (*Flakkorps*) surprisingly did not exist before the beginning of the Second World War, and when they were eventually formed on 3 October 1939, only two units, Flak Corps I and Flak Corps II, existed. They had three main purposes: anti-aircraft, anti-tank and operations that required heavy fire support.

Flak corps varied in their makeup and included different numbers of anti-aircraft regiments, brigades or divisions. Somewhat remarkably these units remained the only two that were formed, until the latter stages of the war. Flak Corps III was not formed until February 1944 and was deployed in different locations throughout Europe. They took part in trying to hold the Allies at bay during the Normandy landings, where they deployed some 12,000 men, who between them manned twenty-seven heavy batteries and twenty-six light batteries.

Flak Corps IV came into being in July 1944, in support of Germany Army Group O, as they fought to try and halt the Allies in their advance across Europe. The Flak corps were highly respected by Allied intelligence, who in 1943 wrote the following brief report about them.

The Flak Corps is a wartime organisation and constitutes an operational reserve of the commander

*in chief of the German Air Force. It combines great
mobility with heavy fire power. It can be employed in
conjunction with spearheads composed of armoured
and motorised forces, and with non-motorized troops
in forcing river crossings and attacking fortified
positions. It can also be deployed as highly mobile
artillery to support tank attacks.*

One of the most recognisable anti-aircraft weapons of the
Second World War was undoubtedly the German 88mm
anti-aircraft and anti-tank artillery gun. The word *Flak*
comes from the German word *Flugzeugabwehrkanone*,
which in English means aircraft-defence cannon, an accurate
description of its use. The abbreviation 'Flak' then became
the generic term in English when referring to anti-aircraft
gun batteries. A reference often heard in historical terms to
describe such a weapon was an *Acht-Acht* (Eight-Eight) gun.

The anti-aircraft defence of Germany after 1935 did not
come under the control of the Wehrmacht – the German
Army – but the Luftwaffe. At the outbreak of war Germany
had stockpiled some 6,700 light flak guns and 2,628 heavy
flak guns, and although this was twice as many heavy anti-
aircraft guns as Great Britain had, it would turn out to be
nowhere near the amount she needed to effectively safeguard
the nation's cities. This subject is discussed elsewhere in the
book in more detail.

The 88mm gun turned out to be an extremely flexible
weapon. In photographs it is often seen on its wheels, more

often than not when it was being used as an improvised anti-tank gun, or in an emplaced position when it was used for its original purpose, as an anti-aircraft gun.

A staggering fact about the 88mm guns was the amount of money that was spent on producing them, which was more about the number that were built rather than the cost of actually making them. In January 1943 it is reported that Germany was spending some 39 million Reichsmarks on anti-aircraft defences, whilst the rest of its entire defence budget, for all three arms of its military, was 93 million Reichsmarks. This was a cost that was more about necessity than desire, as Germany struggled to deal with an ever-increasing bombing campaign by both the Royal Air Force and the United States Air Force.

The 88mm gun was by far the most important anti-aircraft weapon that Germany built during the Second World War. The heavy flak version of it came in four different variants, the most popular being the 8.8cm Flak 18/36/37, of which more than 20,000 were built during the war. It was a truly formidable weapon, loved by those who used it, and feared even more by those whom it was used against. Even today, it is the type of weapon that people look at in amazement. It was far beyond anything that Britain or America had in their armouries and remains today a truly iconic weapon of its time.

During the Battle of France in 1940, the 88mm gun was deployed to support the infantry in the form of twenty-four mixed Flak battalions. It was such a powerful weapon that at a distance of 2km it could penetrate over 84mm thick armour. During the same battle, it was responsible for destroying 152 tanks and 151 bunkers.

Although it was responsible for shooting down hundreds of RAF and USAAF bombers, it got to a stage in the latter part of the war – certainly by the beginning of 1944 – when regardless of how good a weapon it was, it had almost become ineffective, not because of any internal failings, but because of what it was up against. The RAF and the USAAF were attacking German cities around the clock – America during the day and Britain throughout the hours of darkness. It was relentless, and this was not just a case of ten or twenty aircraft being involved in these raids, the war had moved on and it was the time of the 'Thousand-bomber raids', and with each aircraft that made it through the outer ring of anti-aircraft batteries and fighter aircraft, the payload that they delivered on their intended targets brought death and misery to the civilian population and caused utter devastation to homes and businesses.

It was felt by some in the German military that the massive Allied bombing raids had made the 88mm gun almost obsolete; it was no longer cost effective to carry on manufacturing it and that the money saved could be better spent on other, much needed items of military hardware.

During the Second World War, there were only two German cities that were deemed worthy enough by the Nazis to need Flak Towers or *Flakturm*. They were Berlin, which had three and Hamburg, which had two. These were very impressive structures resembling large forts. The original towers were some 128 feet in height, measuring 231 feet by 231 feet, and were made of reinforced concrete, with walls that were anywhere up to 11 feet thick. Hitler had ordered their construction after the RAF carried out a bombing raid on Berlin in 1940, and each of them were erected in just six months. Like everything else, these Flak Towers evolved over time, although those that followed were noticeably smaller than their original counterparts.

The central structures of these towers were so big that they could house 10,000 local civilians during an air raid. They even contained a hospital ward. Besides anti-aircraft guns, they also housed a radar installation and a radar dish, which when required could be retracted behind a concrete and steel dome for protection. Those who designed and built the towers were of the belief that they were so solid they could withstand a direct hit from ordnance dropped from an RAF bomber; how much of that belief was built on fact or fiction is unknown.

The gunners who manned these Flak Towers could sustain a fire power of some 8,000 rounds per minute from their multi-level guns. Their smaller weapon, the 2cm Flak 30, had an effective range of nearly 9 miles, and could be used in a 360-degree field of fire. In relation to the British and American heavy bombers that more often than not were used to raid Berlin, the Germans tended to use the 128mm guns, as it enabled them to engage the raiding aircraft whilst they were still some distance away from the city.

Not one of these towers, either in Berlin, Hamburg or in Vienna was destroyed during the war. In fact, when the Russians finally took Berlin, they found that they could not demolish the towers, even with their massive 203mm howitzers, so they had to send a group of soldiers to approach the towers to get those inside to surrender. Because of their size they were able to be fully stocked with food, stores and ammunitions, which added to their impregnability.

In Berlin the three-tower complex consisted of a *Leitturm*, or Lead Tower, which was the main command tower. The skies would have been searched for incoming bombers who were en route to the city. They would have been where listening for the aircraft was carried out. Their armaments would have usually consisted of forty, (ten quadruple) mounted 20mm guns. The other towers were the *Gefechtsturm*, or Combat Tower, from where the main anti-aircraft firing was done. These usually had as their armaments eight, four-twinned 128 Flak 40mm guns, along with numerous 37mm and thirty-two eight quad-mounted 20mm guns. The configuration of different weapons systems changed as the newer designed towers came into use.

Flakturm I was situated at Berlin Zoo, which is in the Tiergarten. The *Gefechtsturm* was demolished by the British Army at the end of the war. It was a notable structure that withstood everything that both the RAF and the USAAF could throw at it, although British and American aircraft did tend to steer well clear of the towers, as getting too close to them would have been suicidal.

Flakturm II was situated at Friedrichshain in Berlin. The *Leitturm* was also demolished by the British Army after the war.

Flakturm III was situated in Humboldthain Park in Berlin. Both the *Gefechtsturm* and the *Leitturm* were partly destroyed by the British Army at the end of the war. The reason why they were only partially demolished was simply an example of how well constructed the buildings were.

Flakturm IV was situated at Heiligengeistfeld in Hamburg. The *Leitturm* was demolished by the British Army after the war, whilst the *Gefechtsturm* became, of all things, a night club, music school and shops. The size of the structure was highlighted with its six levels, not including the roof.

Flakturm VI was situated at Wilhelmsburg, Hamburg. The *Leitturm* was demolished by the British Army after the end of the war, and the *Gefechtsturm* is still a structure in Hamburg today, albeit renovated and slighted jazzed up.

Flakturms V, VII, and VIII, were in Vienna, with all six towers still intact. The *Gefechtsturm* in the Stiftskaserne district of Vienna, is in use by the Austrian Army. There were plans to build three more towers in Berlin, two in Bremen, one in Hamburg, eight in Munich, and three in Vienna, but none of them were ever built.

There were three main weapons used by the German anti-aircraft batteries. The 37mm Flak 43, the 2cm Gebirgsflak 38, and the 12.8cm Flak 40. The 37mm Flak evolved throughout the war. It started with the 37mm Flak 18, and went on to 36, 37 and 43 variations, and saw service throughout the Second World War. It was an effective anti-aircraft weapon for aircraft that flew under a ceiling of 4,200m. Beyond that it was not of much use.

It had a rate of fire of 120 rounds per minute, which was not particularly high for use as an anti-aircraft weapon. By the time it had evolved to the 3.7cm Flak 43 version, it had a gas operated breech system, which was deemed to be a big improvement on previous models, although its rate of fire had only marginally increased to 150 rounds per minute. There was a variation of this, the 3.7cm Flakzwilling 43, a twin gun mount design, that someone in the team had failed to work out would make the gun very top heavy, which made it somewhat unstable and affected the accuracy of the weapon.

The 3.7cm Flak 37 and the Flak 43 versions were often used mounted on the back or top of a vehicle. By way of example, the Flak 37 was synonymous with its use in conjunction with the *Sonderkraftfahrzeug*, which in English translates to 'special purpose vehicle'. It was better known by the abbreviation Sd.Kfz.7, which was a half-track vehicle used by the Wehrmacht, Luftwaffe and Waffen SS. The Sd.Kfz.7 was also used to transport the 88mm anti-aircraft gun.

The 2cm Gebirgsflak 30 and 38, were 20mm anti-aircraft weapons deployed by various German units throughout the Second World War. It was used in different modes, including in a static position, on the back of a four-wheeled vehicle, or in a two-wheeled version which could be towed into position and coupled to a vehicle. It was also produced in different variants, with the most famous version being the *Flakvierling 38*, which combined the weapon's iconic four Flak auto-cannons into one single barrel. It became the most single mass-produced piece of German artillery during the Second World War.

Germany had produced Flak guns towards the end of the First World War, but due to the restrictions placed upon her by the Treaty of Versailles, she was forbidden from keeping them. The Second World War version of this weapon, the 2cm Flak 30, was multi-functional, and used by the Army, the Kriegsmarine, for anti-aircraft purposes, and the Luftwaffe, which was in charge of anti-aircraft batteries. It was also experimented with as a weapon to be used on board Heinkel He 112s.

The fundamental problem with the weapon, especially when taking in to account its main purpose, was its rate of fire. It could only manage 120 rounds per minute, which for an anti-aircraft weapon, trying to shoot fast-moving enemy aircraft out of the skies, was not particularly fast. The makers of the weapon upgraded it with the 2cm Flak 30 version, which greatly increased its rate of fire to 220 rounds per minute, and at the outbreak of the war it was the standard weapon of choice for both the Army (*Heer*) and the Kriegsmarine.

The Germans wanted to improve the weapon, but also to make it lighter, so they changed the manufacturer and awarded the contract to Mauser, who came up with the 2cm Gebirgsflak 38, with its main feature being that it sat on a mount, held off the ground by a tripod. It was 1942 before the weapon eventually came into service.

Different ammunition was used with the 2cm Flak gun, which was designed to react in different ways. The HE-T round had a nose-fused tracer round, which would self-destruct after five and a half seconds due to tracer burn through. It was intended for firing at aircraft that were flying at a very high altitude. It is hard not to imagine the effect one of those rounds would have on the human body if a flyer was shot with one before it had detonated. Most of the variations either had a nose or base fuse that would self-destruct after a matter of seconds, although one of them was designed to self-destruct at a height of 2 kilometres.

The 12.8cm Flak 40 and its variant types, including the 12.8 Flak Flakzwilling 40/2, and the 12.8cm PaK 40, was one of the most effective heavy anti-aircraft guns of any participant nation during the Second World War. A massive weapon weighing nearly 12 tonnes, it was so heavy that the early versions had to have the barrel removed when it was being transported. It was built by Rheinmetall-Borsig GmbH, a European defence contractor still in existence today, and successfully completed its testing in the latter stages of 1937, two years before the outbreak of the war, providing plenty of opportunity for the Army to become proficient in its use.

The next version of the gun went into production in 1942, by which time its use had been refined from its previous mobile existence to a weapon that would always be used in a static position, bolted into a concrete base. If the original version was classed as being a heavy weapon, the new *Flakzwilling* twin gun mount version was an absolute monster. At 26.5 tonnes it weighed more than double that of the original model, but as it was going to be used in a static position, it did not really matter too much. On the fortified anti-aircraft Zoo Tower in Berlin, there were four of these monster weapons, ready and waiting to unload their formidable armaments against British and American aircraft.

During the final death throes of Nazi Germany's Third Reich, when the Russian Army was fighting its way into the city of Berlin, the four 12.8cm Flak 40 guns on the top of the fortified anti-aircraft Zoo Tower were used to great effect, primarily against the Red Army's tanks. The Flak 40 fired a shell that weighed just over 50lb, which was fired with four times as much force than the impressive 88mm Flak 18 and 36 guns. It could fire up to twenty rounds a minute with devastating effect and reportedly knocked out dozens of tanks as Russian forces rushed to capture the Reichstag.

CHAPTER 2

The Butt Report

The Butt Report of 18 August 1941 revealed what had become a really big problem for the RAF's Bomber Command: the inability of their aircraft to carry out effective bombing raids on enemy targets, which in part was down to a combination of the effectiveness of Germany's anti-aircraft batteries, and the fear of them by British pilots and air crews.

In the early stages of the war the only way the Air Ministry had of measuring the success of the air raids carried out by the RAF, was the word of the crews who had flown the missions, and how many of the aircraft either did not return, or did so, but were damaged. Going on the word of the crews alone meant that not only was it an archaic system, but it was one that was open to abuse.

In essence an aircraft could have taken off from its base somewhere in England, made its way across the English Channel, dropping its bombs as it went, flown around France for a couple of hours, then returned to its base. What actually happened on some of these raids was that crews sometimes became confused as to their exact location, especially in the early stages of the war when navigation systems were not so advanced. Inclement weather that left an intended target shrouded in heavy cloud cover was a particular problem, especially if there was no secondary target. The last thing a bomber crew wanted was to be aimlessly flying around close to their intended target, whilst having to dodge German fighter aircraft trying to shoot them out of the skies, and at the same time trying to dodge exploding flak. An empty aircraft, not only because of the reduced weight, but because it no longer had a cargo full of high explosive or incendiary bombs on board, was a slightly safer aircraft for the crew.

The young men who formed the crews of these bombers were very brave individuals. Most were still in their early twenties, if not younger, and although theirs was a dangerous job which they all knew came with the potential for being killed, of course nobody actually wanted to die. Survival and self-preservation are natural and inherent instincts to be found in all of us, and these young men were no different.

To get some clarity on the matter, the Air Ministry decided that they wanted some way of verifying the claims that were being made by the returning crews. This came about because David Bensusan-Butt, a civil servant in the War Cabinet Secretariat, was tasked with reviewing 633 photographs of air raids, and comparing them with the written reports made by the crews who had taken the photographs.

A quick précis of Butt's report strongly suggests that roughly only one third of the crews who claimed to have reached their intended targets actually did so, which means that if Butt's assessment of what he saw in the photographs was correct, it implied that two thirds of the crews lied, or were economical with the truth, about what they did when involved in a raid. Butt's report only included aircraft that had actually jettisoned their bombs, with the three usual reasons for not doing so being bad weather, equipment failure, or enemy action.

Butt's report came up with four main conclusions:

(1) Of those aircraft recorded as attacking their target, only one in three of them actually got within 5 miles of it.

(2) Over the French ports, the proportion was two in three; over Germany as a whole, the proportion was one in four, whilst over the Ruhr specifically, it was only one in ten.

(3) When there was a full moon, the proportion was two in five, in the new moon it was one in fifteen.

(4) All these figures relate only to aircraft recorded as attacking their intended target; the proportion of the total sorties which reached within 5 miles, is less than one-third.

These are absolutely staggering figures. No wonder the German anti-aircraft batteries felt that they were doing so well to combat the threat posed by the RAF. Subsequent reports concluded that in the year between May 1940 and May 1941, a mind boggling 49 per cent of bombs dropped by

Bomber Command fell in open country, nowhere near their intended target. This means that either the crews could not see their intended target because of cloud cover, that they had a very bad bomb aimer, or they jettisoned their bombs intentionally in open country, for a reason only the crews would be aware of.

When everything had been finalised in Butt's report, one of the facts that came out between May 1940 and May 1941, was that only about 5 per cent of British bombers setting out from England on a bombing raid to a target somewhere in occupied Europe, managed to drop their bombs within 5 miles of their intended target. With that in mind, is it any wonder that certain targets had to be repeatedly attacked to put them out of action?

Understandably, when Butt's report came out and the truth about early bombing raids had been laid bare, everybody was shocked at what was referred to as the 'failure of Bomber Command'. War by its very nature requires certain information to be kept between a select few individuals on a need-to-know basis, but when it appears that a big lie has taken place and a cover-up then followed, people were not usually very impressed at all.

Sadly, rather than senior RAF commanders accepting the findings of Butt's report and moving forward in a positive way to try and rectify its failings, they responded by 'closing ranks' and claimed that the statistics in Butt's report were incorrect, and then went about commissioning their own report; not as one might hope, by an independent person or group, in an effort to give their findings some credibility, but by the Directorate of Bombing Operations. Despite the obvious conflict of interest that this brought with it, they delivered what was clearly a totally biased report, which in essence came down on the side of Bomber Command. It was quite a confusing report, because it did not so much address the main points that Butt's report had thrown up, but instead came up with some quite bizarre claims about how the RAF could win the war in just six months by bombing the forty-three German towns and cities that had populations of more than 100,000, with 4,000 bombers.

These were points that were not even raised in Butt's report. How the RAF came up with their figures, and how they could support them with any solid facts, was not explained. Despite the claims having been made by Sir Charles Portal, the Chief of the Air Staff, not everybody was convinced by them, including Winston Churchill. There was still no 'give' from the RAF's hierarchy, instead they became even more entrenched in their opinion, claiming that even if they did not knock Germany out of the war in the time scale they had mentioned, their efforts would sufficiently weaken the enemy to allow the British Army back into Europe where they would quickly gain a foothold. Not everybody was in agreement or understood what the strategic bombing policy actually was. It was ironic that the very failings of Bomber Command's strategy around the issue of precision bombing, provided them with the very 'ammunition' they needed to argue their case to commence a strategy of 'area bombing'.

Their case was greatly assisted by what was known as the 'dehousing paper', a report produced by Lord Cherwell on 30 March 1942, which proposed and supported the idea of Bomber Command carrying out a strategy of area bombing rather than continuing with what he referred to as the futile attempts at precision bombing. Such a policy was certainly not good for Germany's anti-aircraft defences, which, within reason, could work out the potential buildings, facilities, factories and military targets that they best needed to defend. What they could not possibly know was what they were soon to be confronted with.

Despite the support from Lord Cherwell, some high-ranking military personnel, especially those from the Army and Navy, were not happy with what they saw as the disproportionate allocation of resources of both manpower and materials that the RAF, and Bomber Command in particular, were being given, to the detriment of their own services. It was harder for them to take because of the notion that regardless of how many raids Bomber Command carried out, there was very little to show for it that was tangible and justified a continuation of the strategy.

The Navy had their say in the matter as well, when Professor Blackett, the Royal Navy's Chief Scientist, challenged some of Lord Cherwell's claims, and even wrote to him pointing this out, stating that he was concerned that if he, Cherwell, stuck to his figures, which according to Professor Blackett were far from being correct, the War Office would make a wrong decision based on incorrect information.

To clear up the ambiguity, the War Cabinet asked High Court Judge Mr Justice Singleton, to look at the differing views. In essence, he came down on the side of Bomber Command, which saw the area bombing directive issued on 14 February 1942, and just eight days later, Air Chief Marshal Sir Arthur Travers 'Bomber' Harris becoming the new Air Officer Commanding-in-Chief of Bomber Command.

The Area Bombing Directive was issued to the RAF by the Government's Air Ministry on 14 February 1942 and greatly changed not only how British bombers would attack their targets, but it also made matters slightly more difficult for Germany's anti-aircraft batteries. The direct targeting of civilians had been something which Germany and Britain had purposely steered away from when carrying out air raids on each other, maybe in the forlorn hope that they could eventually become allies, although it was not a tactic that the Germans had employed when they invaded Poland.

A report had been presented to the British Cabinet by Professor Frederick Lindemann, the government's leading scientific adviser, in the early days of February 1942. It looked at how best to affect enemy war production. Lindemann's suggestion was that the RAF should carry out attacks on German cities where there were major industrial areas. Besides this, part of his plan was also to destroy German homes, so as to displace workers and reduce their ability to work, which in turn affected German production of much-needed military hardware and equipment. The job of making this happen, was given to 'Bomber' Harris.

Although both Britain and Germany had begun the war in a more conciliatory manner when it came to bombing each other, with a major consideration being not to target each other's civilian population, this changed as the war progressed and precision targeting was replaced with area bombing, which included civilian areas.

This change in policy made life a lot more difficult for anti-aircraft batteries. Guarding a building, a factory, or a structure such as a harbour, was relatively straightforward, because what was being protected was a specific area, and a relatively small area at that. But when it came to the bombing of civilian areas, it was a whole new ball game, and one that was hard to prevent. If the Allied bombers had not been stopped before they reached their intended target, which the Luftwaffe could only guess at, then it was nigh on impossible to stop the bombers from releasing their payload of bombs. If, say, 200 aircraft were involved in the raid and the anti-aircraft batteries and fighter aircraft managed to account for 50 of the aircraft, that still left 150 of them which could then drop their bombs with devastating effect.

As if Germany wasn't having a difficult enough time in defending her country against the persistence of the Royal Air Force bombing raids on her major cities, things became a whole lot worst once the Americans entered the war. Now it was the additional bombing power of the Flying Fortresses that their anti-aircraft defences had to contend with. It must have been disheartening and demoralising for the German defenders.

America's first raid of the European war took place on 27 January 1943, when Flying Fortress bombers took part in a raid on the German submarine base at Wilhelmshaven. There were similar structures at Bremen, Danzig, Hamburg, Heligoland and Kiel, all in Germany, as well as at Bordeaux, Brest, La Rochelle, Lorient and St Nazaire in France and Bergen and Trondheim in Norway, all of which would have had anti-aircraft defensive units in place for protection against similar raids.

Once America became involved in bombing occupied Europe, the world must have changed radically for the German people. Now they were being bombed day and night on a regular basis – by the Americans during the day and the British at night. When taking into account the damage these continual raids were having on Germany's war manufacturing capacity, it is truly amazing that she managed to stay in the war for so long. Any premises or location that the Allies could link to being of use to the German war effort was bombed: aircraft factories, submarine bases, ball bearing factories, dams in the Ruhr valley, coke works, steel works, armaments and aircraft factories.

It became all-out war when the British RAF, under the leadership of 'Bomber' Harris, and on the advice and suggestion of government, changed the policy of precision bombing to area bombing, which gave bomber crews the go ahead to target what were known to be civilian areas. This was done to affect German morale with thousands of civilians being killed and wounded and even more who had become displaced and were refugees in their own country.

There was also the knock-on effect of soldiers who were away from home fighting in the war and who were now worried about their loved ones back home, not knowing if they were alive or dead because of the constant bombing being undertaken by the Allies all across Germany.

CHAPTER 3

German Successes

The following is a wartime list of the successes of German air defences protecting the capital city of Berlin; but this is more about the skill and determination of the anti-aircraft batteries on the ground than the pilots deployed in the air. As the tactics of conducting air raids over enemy territory changed, so the ground forces lying in wait for them became less effective, because the main change in bomber aircraft carrying out raids was that there were more of them on each raid, which made it impossible for anti-aircraft batteries to shoot down or damage as many of the raiding aircraft, although they did their best in the circumstances.

1939

4 September: Five Bristol Blenheim bomber aircraft and three Vickers Wellington long range medium bombers were shot down through a combination of Messerschmitt Bf 109s and flak from 88mm anti-aircraft guns.

1941

7 November: RAF Bomber Command launched a massive raid on Berlin with over 160 of its aircraft. A total of 21 of them were shot down or crashed, as the capital city defended itself.

The Nazis were many things, most of which do not need any reference in the pages of this book, but they were far from stupid. The epicentre of the Third Reich was Berlin, so it went without saying that in the minds of the German people, if the Nazis couldn't protect them in their nation's capital, how could they ever hope to protect them? So, with this in mind, the Nazis came up with a plan. They knew that even in a worst-case scenario, it would be a long time before enemy soldiers ever got to walk through the streets of Berlin, but they also knew that the first attacks on their capital would be by air.

As early as 1937, two years before the outbreak of the war, air raid drills were carried out in the central government district of Berlin, which included the Reich Chancellery. There was an official policy for how the air raid drills should be carried out, which in part read as follows:

> *To carry out the air raid drills, a precise regulation is required for the three office buildings, Wilhelmstrasse 77, Wilhelmstrasse 78 and Voss Strasse 1 ... The officials and residents of Wilhelmstrasse 78 and Voss Strasse 1 can go to the substitute shelters in Wilhelmstrasse 78 and Voss*

Strasse 1. The inhabitants of the Reich Chancellor House, Wilhelmstrasse 77, will use the shelter under the ballroom.

The somewhat comical charade of that order, intended or otherwise, was that the only residents of Willhelmstrasse 77 were Adolf Hitler, his staff, bodyguards and servants.

In Berlin many of the *U-Bahn* stations, the equivalent of railway stations, were also converted into shelters. The plan, even before the outbreak of the war, was to build some 2,000 air raid shelters in the nation's capital, but something went wrong and only 300 of them were built. Why is not clear, as it certainly would not have been for financial reasons, as money would not have been an issue for a free spending Nazi party. By 1941 there was progress at last with the building of five massive shelters for public use in the event of an air raid. Their names were Zoo, Anhalt Station, Humboldthain, Friedrichshain and Kleistpark. They were collectively large enough to cater for 65,000 people, but this wasn't all. Another scheme saw similar air raid shelters built beneath government buildings, including one under the Reich Chancellery often referred to as the *Führerbunker* and one underneath the old Reich Chancellery, known as the *Vorbunker*, which was originally intended as an air raid shelter for Adolf Hitler and his entourage of guards and servants.

Between 1940 and 1945, Berlin was attacked by the RAF's Bomber Command, whose aircraft dropped a total of 45,517 tons of bombs on the beleaguered city. In addition, the USAAF Eighth Air Force carried out attacks between

1943 and 1945 when they dropped 23,000 tons of bombs. The French Air Force did the same between 1944 and 1945, and finally, during the Battle of Berlin, Russia did the same as her ground troops fought their way into the centre of Berlin. In total the capital of a slowly crumbling Germany had been subjected to 363 air raids.

The largest of these raids by the Americans took place on the afternoon of 3 February 1945, when nearly 1,000 B-17 Flying Fortresses of the USAAF Eighth Air Force, with protection provided by 575 P-51 Mustangs, attacked the area of the Berlin railway system. This resulted in a fire which spread eastwards and continued for four days before it burnt itself out.

Here is a list of the dates of the air raids that the Allies undertook against Berlin:

7/8 June 1940. A French Navy long-range transport aircraft dropped bombs on the capital. This was the first air attack on Berlin during the Second World War.

25/26 August 1940. Ninety-five aircraft from the RAF's Bomber Command attacked Berlin, the raid beginning at 12.20pm. This was a significant raid because the people of Berlin had been told by their leaders that no enemy aircraft would ever manage to get through the city's inner and outer rings of anti-aircraft defences. Despite a crescendo of noise and a light show to behold as the anti-aircraft batteries opened fire on the enemy they could hear but not see, their efforts were ultimately ineffective. Not only were no aircraft shot down, but the German searchlights did not pick up a single allied bomber in their beams. Nobody was killed in the raid, and only minor damage was caused to a small number of buildings, but the overall achievement was the damage that had been caused to the morale of the German people, who realised that what they had been told by their Nazi leaders was no more than a giant lie.

7 September 1940. The RAF caused damage to the iconic Brandenburg Gate as well as the Christuskirche Church in a raid on Berlin, one which was far more damaging than the German newspapers were allowed to report. The same day saw German bombers carry out a raid on London.

24 March 1941. A mixed force of 130 bombers from the RAF and No.300 Squadron of the Polish Air Force took part in a raid on a heavily defended Berlin.

8 September 1941. An attack by the RAF was made on the Potsdamer Bahnhof, a Berlin railway station, which resulted in the deaths of more than 100 German civilians.

7/8 November 1941. This attack by 160 aircraft of Bomber Command was not their finest hour. Twenty crews were lost, mainly to anti-aircraft fire, and only about 30 per cent of the aircraft actually reached their intended target area. Because of heavy cloud cover the effectiveness of the subsequent bombing was minimal, as the bombs were dropped across a wide area.

2 March 1943. An attack by 251 aircraft saw a total of 610 tons of bombs dropped on the German capital. The city's anti-aircraft gunners managed to shoot down 17 of the attacking aircraft, but the losses amongst the German civilian population were staggering, with 711 killed. In a sad irony of that same day, 1,500 Jewish men who had been rounded up three days earlier were deported from Berlin and sent by train to Auschwitz. Of these, 1,350 were murdered upon their arrival at the camp.

23/24 August 1943. A mixture of 727 Lancaster, Halifax, Stirling and Mosquito aircraft left the UK to carry out a raid on Berlin, but 70 of them had to turn back before they reached their target. By the time the raid was over, the RAF had lost 57 of its aircraft, most of which had been brought down by anti-aircraft fire in and around the German capital. An Avro-Lancaster from No.103 2nd Squadron, with the serial number W4364 and the name *Billie*, which took part in the raid, became the first Lancaster bomber to complete fifty successful sorties. Sadly, four days later it was lost in a raid on Nuremberg.

31 August/1 September 1943. Bomber Command sent 613 heavy bombers, accompanied by 9 Mosquitos, to bomb Berlin. They met a determined resistance, which resulted in 47 aircraft being destroyed marking another successful night's work for Berlin's anti-aircraft crews.

3/4 September 1943. On this night 316 Lancaster bombers, along with 4 Mosquitos, headed for Berlin to lay a number of diversionary flares to distract the city's defences. The Berlin anti-aircraft gunners shot down 22 of the RAF's planes. One of the aircraft on the raid that night was part of No.207 Squadron, a Lancaster bomber, EM-F. On board the aircraft was the BBC correspondent, Wynford Vaughan

Thomas and sound engineer Reginald Pidsley, who recorded a running commentary of the raid, which was played on BBC radio some twelve hours after it was recorded.

The latter part of November 1943 saw Berlin's anti-aircraft batteries pushed to their limits, as the RAF carried out six raids on the city in quick succession.

18/19 November 1943. Berlin was once again the main target as it was attacked by 444 aircraft, although it was helped somewhat by heavy cloud cover. By way of a diversionary raid, a further 395 bombers attacked the German cities of Mannheim and Ludwigshafen, which sit opposite each other on the river Rhine. By the end of the raids, 32 RAF bombers had been lost, most to the ground fire of the anti-aircraft gunners.

22/23 November 1943. Out of all of the raids on Berlin, this one would go down as the worst as far as the city and its people were concerned. A total of 764 RAF bombers, including 440 Lancasters, were unleashed on Germany's capital. Most of the damage which resulted from the raid was caused to the largely residential areas of Tiergarten, Charlottenburg, Schöneberg, and Spandau. The raid had taken place during a period of relatively good weather, especially for the time of year, and resulted in several firestorms. As a result of the damage caused to their properties 175,000 people were left homeless, and the Kaiser Wilhelm Memorial Church, which was also damaged in the raid, was never repaired, but is to this day a monument to that raid and a tourist attraction in Berlin. The British, French, Italian and Japanese embassies were all substantially damaged, as were Charlottenburg Castle and Berlin Zoo. The Ministry of Weapons and munitions, the Waffen SS Administrative College, along with the barracks of the Imperial Guard at Spandau, were all badly damaged as well as several factories employed in manufacturing items for the German war effort. From an Allied perspective, the raid was an extremely productive night's work, although at the cost of 26 aircraft and the crews who flew them, which were shot down by anti-aircraft gunners.

23/24 November 1943. With the fires still smouldering amongst the wrecked homes and buildings in the centre of Berlin, the RAF attacked the capital again the next day. This time with 383 of bombers. If the residents of Berlin hadn't already received the message that they were not safe in their own homes, and that the Allied bombers could reach them whenever they wanted to, then this raid was intended as a reminder.

24/25 November 1943. It is not absolutely clear what the purpose of this raid was for. The previous two on the city had seen hundreds of RAF bombers drop their ordnance on the stricken capital, but this time there were just six, and one of them was shot down by the city's anti-aircraft gunners.

25/26 November 1943. This raid was even more bizarre. Only three Mosquito bombers made the trip this time, so what its purpose was, and if it actually achieved anything, is unclear.

26/27 November 1943. The night after three Mosquitos attacked Berlin, a total of 450 Lancaster and Mosquito bombers ramped up the pressure on the beleaguered Nazi leadership. This time the main focus of the air raid was the industrial suburb of Reinickendorf in the northwest of the city. A further 84 aircraft attacked Stuttgart as a diversionary manoeuvre. In total the RAF lost 34 of their aircraft that evening. Once again, despite the efforts by the Berlin anti-aircraft gunners, the majority of the British bombers made it to their target.

2/3 December 1943. The myth surrounding Nazi Germany's impregnability had by now been well and truly dispelled, as 425 Lancasters, 18 Mosquitos and 15 Halifax bombers made their way to Berlin to complete yet another air raid on the capital. Unfortunately for the RAF, the Germans discovered they were on their way to Berlin and had sufficient time to scramble their fighters in readiness for their arrival. One of the aircraft lost that night was from No.460 Squadron, an Australian unit, which had two newspaper reporters on board, one being Captain Grieg of the *Daily Mail*.

That evening was not good weather wise and strong cross winds altered the bomber formations making them easier targets for the German defenders. However, they still managed to cause a sufficient amount of damage to two Siemens (at the time known as Siemens-Schucker) factories, several railway installations, and a ball-bearing factory. By the end of the raid the RAF had lost 40 of its bombers and their crews, shot down by either German fighters or anti-aircraft batteries.

16/17 December 1943. The RAF sent 483 Lancaster and 15 Mosquito bombers on the raid that evening. A lot of damage was done to the Berlin railway system, so much so that some 1,000 wagons loaded with equipment and other war material destined for the Eastern Front were delayed for six days. A building which housed Germany's military and political records, and the National Theatre were both destroyed. The RAF lost 25 of its aircraft shot down over Berlin by a mixture of German fighters and anti-aircraft fire. However, the real tragedy was that the raid cost the lives of 328 aircrew, when 29 of the aircraft which made it back crashed due to low cloud whilst attempting to land at their bases, killing more than 150 of the crew.

23/24 December 1943. This saw 379 RAF aircraft on another bombing mission to Berlin. Damage caused by the air raid was comparatively minor, mainly because of heavy cloud over the city, and 16 of the Lancaster Bombers were shot down. To help the raid, there was a diversionary attack carried out by Mosquito bombers at Leipzig.

29/30 December 1943. This very large-scale attack on Berlin involved 712 RAF bombers. Diversionary raids to throw the Germans off the scent of the intended target were carried out over Düsseldorf, Leipzig and Magdeburg. The tactic worked and meant that when the main raiding group arrived over Berlin, they were met with very few enemy fighters. This could also have been because of the very heavy cloud cover of the German capital. Twenty aircraft were lost on the raid over Berlin, most of which were brought down by flak.

1/2 January 1944. The beginning of a new year saw no respite for Berliners, who received the same treatment they had been getting for months. This time it came in the shape of 421 Lancaster bombers, but they didn't have things entirely their own way. A combination of German fighter aircraft and anti-aircraft fire brought down 28 Lancasters. With the standard crew of a Lancaster bomber being 7 men, that meant 196 lost their lives. Losing so many friends and colleagues, who only a few hours before had been alive and well, must have been a hard knock to take.

2/3 January 1944. The following night saw yet another raid on Berlin, when 383 RAF aircraft made their way to the enemy capital without incident. A combination of German fighters and anti-aircraft flak changed all that as soon as they arrived, and 27 of the raiding aircraft were brought down, with the loss of another 189 men.

20/21 January 1944. Since the raid on Berlin on the night of 2/3 January, there had been three further minor raids on the German capital, at least one of which was a diversionary one. There weren't many evenings when the crews and gunners of Berlin's anti-aircraft batteries weren't called into action. A massive raid took place on this evening with 769 bombers taking part in the attack. Losses were 13 Lancasters and 22 Halifax bombers – in human terms 245 men.

27/28 January 1944. A total of 530 RAF bombers, including 515 Lancasters, attacked Berlin in what was only a diversionary raid. It proved to be costly as 33 Lancasters were brought down either by Germany's dwindling number of fighter aircraft, or Berlin's over-worked anti-aircraft batteries. A total of 231 British airmen lost their lives.

28/29 January 1944. The next day Berlin was the target for the RAF's bombers once again, but this time they sent even more aircraft to fill the night skies when 432 Lancasters, 241 Halifaxes and 4 Mosquito bombers made their way to the heart of the city. German fighter aircraft provided a welcome committee and by the time the raid was over, 20 Lancaster and 26 Halifax bombers had been shot down by a combination of fighters and anti-aircraft batteries, but that still left 631 bombers to carry on the raid. Once again, the biggest loss for the British was manpower; in this raid they lost another 322 experienced pilots, navigators, wireless operators, flight engineers, tail gunners and bomb aimers, men who were not easily replaceable. There were two different versions of the attack. Bomber Command claimed that it was one of the most concentrated attacks they had ever carried out on Berlin, whilst the German authorities claimed that the southern and western areas of the city were hit, as well as 77 other places outside the city.

30/31 January 1944. The relentless raids on Berlin continued with 534 aircraft on this night resulting in 33 aircraft being shot down by either anti-aircraft fire or German night fighters. This meant another 245 more men had been killed. Unusually for such a large bomber group, there was no diversionary raid that evening to keep the Germans guessing as to where the British aircraft were heading. Since 20 January 1944, the RAF had now lost nearly 1,000 men killed in the raids over Germany, which was not a rate they would be able to sustain for a prolonged period of time.

15/16 February 1944. Despite there being cloud cover over Berlin, it was once again a target for the RAF. This time they sent 891 aircraft. This was the largest raiding party that the RAF sent anywhere throughout the entire war. It included 561 Lancaster and 314 Halifax aircraft, which were picked up by German radar soon after leaving the British coast. The German fighters were ordered not to fly over the centre of Berlin, but to leave the skies clear for the anti-aircraft batteries. Not all the fighters did as they were requested, and some attacked the British bombers over Berlin. By the time the raid was over 26 Lancaster and 17 Halifax aircraft had been shot down by the German fighters and anti-aircraft batteries. Whether any of the German fighters were shot down by their own batteries is unknown, but it was clearly dangerous for them to ignore an instruction not to follow enemy bombers into the centre of Berlin, knowing that their own ground batteries were going to be opening fire. Once again Berlin was covered by cloud for most of the raid, but this didn't stop the British bombs from hitting their targets, especially in the large industrial area in the Siemensstadt area of the city, with much of what they produced being war related goods. Central and southwestern areas of the city were also damaged.

In a five-day period between 4 and 8 March 1944, American aircraft took over the bombing of Berlin. The raid had been intended to take place on 3 March 1944 but had to be postponed because of bad weather over Berlin, and finally went ahead on 4 March. Most of the raiding party turned back en route due to a recall order, but Colonel Mumford, the commander of the 95th Bomb Group, decided to ignore the order and carried on with the original mission. By the time the raiding party reached Berlin, it consisted of 25 B-17 bombers from the 95th Bomb Group, 9 B-17s from the 100th Bomber Group, and one pathfinder from 382nd Bomb Group. It also included aircraft from the 357th Fighter Group and the 4th Fighter Group who had decided to remain on the raid to escort the bombers of Colonel Mumford. The 95th Bomb Group lost four of its aircraft and the 100th Bomb Group one aircraft. Despite ignoring the recall order, which resulted in 32 American aircraft either shot down by German fighters or anti-aircraft batteries, and more than 50 crewmen being killed, Colonel Mumford was awarded a silver star and the 95th Bomb Group was given a Presidential Unit Citation.

On **6 March**, the Eighth USAAF attacked Berlin with 730 B-17 bombers from 1st, 2nd, and 3rd American Air Divisions. The Americans lost a total of 69 bombers in the attack, along with 11 P-51 Mustang fighters. From the 1st Air Division, 19 aircraft failed to return, which resulted in 60 airmen being killed in action and 117 who were captured and spent the rest of the war as prisoners of war. A number of aircraft crashed on returning to their base, and another crashed shortly after take-off. One aircraft from the 2nd Air Division crashed as it took off, with her tanks full of fuel and a full bomb load she exploded, killing all the crew. Of the aircraft that returned, 8 of the crew members were dead, having been killed in action on the mission, whilst a further 37 had been wounded. From the 242 B-17 aircraft of the 3rd Air Division, 34 failed to return and 3 crash landed, whilst a further 121 had sustained flak and machine-gun damage.

8 March 1944. On this day 623 USAAF bombers carried out yet another raid on Berlin, which resulted in 37 of them, along with 18 fighter aircraft, being shot down, either by anti-aircraft batteries or German defensive fighters. It was an interesting factor of the raids on Berlin that the Americans chose to carry out their raids during the day, while the RAF, who had previously carried out daytime raids, had changed to carrying out raids at night as they felt daytime losses were too heavy.

The night of **24/25 March 1944** became known as 'the night of the strong winds' within Bomber Command. The weather that the bombers experienced was not what had been forecast, instead a powerful northerly wind carried them south at every stage of their journey. It was so strong that the methods in place to warn air crews via their instrument panels of such weather changes did not properly detect their full strength. This resulted in the bomber formation becoming scattered, particularly after the raid was over and the crews were on their way home. This allowed the anti-aircraft batteries to shoot down 72, or nearly 9 per cent, of the RAF's 811 aircraft which took part in the raid. It is believed that 50 of the 72 aircraft that were brought down during the raid were lost due to anti-aircraft fire. Of the 577 Lancaster bombers deployed on the mission, 44 were shot down, and of the 216 Halifax bombers that took part, 28 of them were also shot down, meaning that more than 10 per cent of the crews never made it back home. This was the last major RAF raid on Berlin during the Second World War.

Berlin's anti-aircraft guns did what they could to stand up to the might of the American Flying Fortresses, but ammunition was low and their crews were exhausted, yet despite the overwhelming fire power of what they were up against, they still managed to bring down 36 of the American bombers. One of the pilots who was shot down was Lieutenant-Colonel Robert Rosenthal of the 100th Bombardment Group, and the commanding officer of the First Air Division's bomber force. He survived the aircraft's crash and was captured by the Germans. Despite the efforts of the city's anti-aircraft units, 2,894 civilians were killed in the raid, with a further 20,000 wounded. Because of the destruction the raid caused to civilian housing, 120,000 of Berlin's residents were left homeless.

As Russian forces reached the outskirts of the city in April 1945, the air raids on Berlin ceased. An estimated 20,000 civilians had been killed during the attacks, which, when compared to raids carried out on other German cities, where similar numbers of people had been killed in just one raid, was comparatively low. The relatively low numbers of casualties sustained in Berlin was in part due to the city's excellent air defences, bunkers and air raid shelters, plus the fact that in 1943, the Nazis decided that all non-essential people should be evacuated from Berlin. By 1944 1.2 million people, mostly women and children, had been moved to more rural areas. Despite the large number of evacuees, the city still had a population of some 3.5 million, although by January 1945 this had reduced to somewhere in the region of 2.9 million.

As the war continued, so the age of the Flak gunners became younger. As older men were drafted into the regular Army and sent to the front, it was the youngsters of the Hitler Youth who were increasingly used to man the guns, but by 1945 females from the League of German Girls – also referred to as the Band of German Maidens – were operating the Flak guns. The female version of the Hitler Youth organisation consisted of three sections depending on age. The youngest group were aged between 10 and 14, the main group was for those aged 14 to 18, and the older group for girls up to the age of 21 was voluntary. In a relatively short period of time anti-aircraft batteries had gone from being armed by men, then by boys and then girls. It was an important role and one that could, and did, determine whether somebody lived or died. The situation was exacerbated by the fact that during 1944, as the effectiveness of the Luftwaffe declined, it was unable to provide any significant air support to the Flak and other anti-aircraft ground units that were doing their best to protect Berlin and Germany's other major cities from Allied air raids.

With the war in its final months, and the Allies rapidly fighting their way across Europe from both sides, the world for Adolf Hitler and the rest of the Nazi leadership had become a much smaller place. On 16 January 1945, Hitler moved his headquarters into the *Führerbunker* where, along with a number of top Nazis, he remained until his death on 30 April. The *Vorbunker* was then used as accommodation by a number of top Nazis and other senior military personnel, as well as for food storage.

CHAPTER 4

United States Intelligence Bulletin

Throughout the Second World War the United States War Department printed regular military updates in a publication entitled the Intelligence Bulletin. Its purpose was to inform officers and enlisted men of the latest known tactics being deployed, and the weapons used by German, Japanese and other Axis forces. These bulletins provide a rare insight into what the Allies knew about the forces of the Axis powers.

The edition of the Intelligence Bulletin dated 4 November 1943 included the following two headings, 'Weaknesses of Artillery Defensive Positions' and 'Tactical Employment of Flak in the Field'. The following report concerns Germany's use of both light and heavy anti-aircraft units in the capacity of anti-aircraft, anti-tank and artillery use. The report began with an introduction:

> *The original German doctrine regarding the employ-*
> *ment of German Air Force flak artillery in the field*
> *has steadily been undergoing modification. German*

manuals formerly describing the responsibility of flak in the field as primarily, and almost exclusively, anti-aircraft defense; the engagement of ground targets was regarded as secondary, and only to be undertaken in an emergency. Although the older manuals admitted the possibility of using light flak to reinforce the fire of heavy infantry weapons, and of using heavy flak to supplement anti-tank and other artillery, such employment was described as exceptional. There was nothing to suggest, for example, the now extensive use of the 88-mm anti-aircraft gun in an anti-tank role.

The transition from the defensive doctrine of the earlier manuals to the more aggressive modern conception seems to date from the introduction of the Flak Corps units, which first appeared during the Battle of France. The Flak Corps was created to perform the tasks described in the following enemy notes.

The Flak Corps is a wartime organization and constitutes an operational reserve of the commander in chief of the German Air Force. It combines great mobility with heavy fire power. It can be employed in conjunction with spearheads composed of armoured and motorized forces, and with non-motorized troops in forcing river crossings and attacking fortified positions. It can also be deployed as highly mobile artillery to support tank attacks.

The Flak Corps can take part in anti-tank defense on a broad front and can be employed in ground engagements at strongly contested points. Its capabilities are tremendous in anti-aircraft defense, because its great mobility enables it to rush flak concentrations to strategically important points, and to transfer flak strength from one area to another, as required. It is also responsible for protecting forward ground organizations of the German Air Force.

It can be clearly seen that the Americans fully understood the advantages and effectiveness of Germany's Flak Corps, and the different roles in which it could be deployed.

As these notes show, flak in the field is now intended to serve as a powerful and highly mobile striking force. The emphasis laid on its employment in the ground role, and in an offensive capacity in conjunction with spearhead formations, is most important. Experience has verified that these principles are actively practised in the field.

The bulletin then went on to speak about Germany's premier artillery weapon in some detail: the 88mm gun. Not only was it extremely mobile, but it was universally considered to be the most menacing of artillery pieces used as part of heavy flak and anti-aircraft batteries. Heavier weapons were also used but these could usually only be found where a static target was being defended, such as important government buildings.

The heavy flak battery consists either of four or six guns, which were usually 88mms, along with two light guns, 20 mms, for close protection. Six-gun batteries are becoming increasingly common. In theory the heavy battery consists of two platoons, but in practice it is rarely divided in this manner. All the guns are generally fitted with shields, to protect the detachments against small-arms fire, and with two sights, a telescopic sight for the direct engagement of ground targets, and a panoramic sight for indirect laying. In the interests of mobility, the fire-control equipment is often left behind. In addition to time-fuse high explosive ammunition, armour-piercing and percussion fuse high explosive ammunition is normally carried. To avoid the muzzle flashes which, at night, readily give away the gun positions, the Germans now make widespread use of a flashless propellant.

The 88-mm gun can be put into action in about 2 minutes. If necessary, it can be fired from its mount, but against ground targets only. Since the normal mount is conspicuous because of its height, the gun is extremely vulnerable to artillery fire. Whenever possible, therefore, the gun is dug in so that only the barrel appears over the top of the emplacement.

Actually, the time factor and the frequent moves do not always permit the Germans to devise effective concealment. Realizing that destruction of hostile observation posts constitutes an indirect method of protecting their heavy flak guns, the Germans try to accomplish this at every opportunity.

German air defence units were usually deployed with either a command device, known in German as a *Kommandogerät*, which was a fire control computer, or a portable Wurzburg radar. The use of either of these devices greatly helped with the high level of accuracy of an 88mm gun against enemy aircraft.

A Würzburg radar, named after the German city of Würzburg, was a low-level UHF band radar. It was the main ground-based gun-laying radar that was used by the Wehrmacht, Luftwaffe and German Army. Although its initial development began before the war, it did not come into use until 1940, with over 4,000 models being produced before the end of the war.

The report continued:

Employment in Rear Areas

In rear areas heavy flak has the normal task of providing anti-aircraft protection for ports, airfields, dumps, headquarters, and points of importance on lines of communication. Predictors and/or auxiliary predictors are employed, and mobile radio-location equipment may also be allotted. Although flak units in rear areas primarily have the task of providing anti-aircraft protection, even these units are normally provided with armour-piercing and percussion-fuse high-explosive ammunition, and therefore can operate against any hostile troops or armoured vehicles which may break through. The heavy flak's degree of preparedness to meet such attacks naturally depends on the distance between the guns and the front.

Employment in Forward Areas

It is in the employment of heavy flak batteries attached to the Army, for operations in forward areas, that current German methods depart most noticeably from the doctrine expressed in earlier manuals. Formerly, German doctrine outlined a primary anti-aircraft role, a secondary anti-tank role, and, under exceptional circumstances, employment in a field-artillery role.

A certain proportion of heavy batteries in forward areas are still deployed in an anti-aircraft role, chiefly to protect forward airfields, and during periods of inactivity or preparation the anti-aircraft role still predominates. For example, an assembly prior to an attack will usually be protected by heavy guns, and under these conditions the ground role is assumed only in the event that the Germans are subjected to a surprise attack. However, once battle is joined, whether in attack or defense and especially when armoured forces are involved, the heavy flak guns are usually employed against ground targets only, and the anti-aircraft role becomes the exception. If necessary, even guns originally deployed to give anti-aircraft protection to forward airfields are sometimes pressed into service as anti-tank weapons.

It is interesting to note how many of these weapons which, although having initially come in to being for use as an anti-aircraft weapon, ended up with a multi-functional purpose, being just as effective in whatever capacity they were deployed.

Light Flak

Light flak units operating in the field are generally equipped with 20mm guns, single or four barrelled, sometimes with 37mm guns, and once in a while with 50mm guns. A light battery normally consists of four platoons of 20mm guns, or three platoons of the larger calibre light guns, with three guns to each platoon.

Light flak guns are especially useful in combatting surprise attacks, because of the rapidity with which these pieces can be put into action. The 20mm Flak 30, for example, can be put into action in about half a minute, and in extreme emergencies all light flak guns can be fired, although with a limited traverse, from their mounts. In addition, it is known that self-propelled models of the 20mm and 37mm calibres exist and can engage both air and ground targets. Like the heavy guns, the light guns in the field are usually fitted with shields for protection against small arms fire. They are also fitted with flak sights and or telescopic or linear sights and carry armour-piercing ammunition in addition to percussion fuse high explosive ammunition. Light flak guns may engage ground targets, especially "soft-skinned" vehicles, at ranges of as much as 800 yards, but are most effective at ranges up to about 300 yards.

Germany had begun the aerial bombing of British cities almost immediately after Britain declared war in September 1939. In response it wasn't until May 1940 that the RAF carried out its first air raid over Germany, targeting oil dumps, train marshalling yards and steelworks, all of which were either military or industrial war related targets.

Britain's policy in relation to conducting bombing missions over Germany changed dramatically throughout the war. To begin with the RAF was forbidden to attack targets in urban areas of Germany because of the possible risk of death to civilians. But as from 9 September 1940, British air crews were told that due to the indiscriminate nature of German bombing of British cities, they were allowed from that day forth to drop their bombs on targets of opportunity rather than return from a mission with a full payload of bombs, if they were unable to find their originally assigned targets.

The Luftwaffe's air raid on Coventry on 14 November 1940 by 515 bombers saw a total of 500 tonnes of high explosive bombs dropped on the city, including 36,000 incendiary devices. Besides the city's buildings and factories that were damaged and destroyed in the raid, some 4,300 of Coventry's homes were also destroyed, which led to an estimated 568 deaths, although the exact figure has never been confirmed. A further 863 civilians were severely wounded with another 383 who sustained minor injuries.

As a direct result of the attack on Coventry, the RAF carried out its first aerial bombing attack on the night of 15/16 December 1940 on the German city of Mannheim, destroying nearly half of it in the process. The gloves were well and truly off on both sides. Britain's initial fair play approach had disappeared to be replaced by a hard-nosed take on the matter of playing Nazi Germany at her own game. When it came to anti-aircraft defensive measures, however, Germany certainly had more time to prepare than Britain did.

Employment in Rear Areas

In rear areas light flak batteries have the normal task of giving anti-aircraft protection to such vital points as airfields, bridges, railroad stations and junctions, headquarters, and depots. For this purpose batteries are generally deployed as a whole, with the guns sited by platoons. Although the anti-aircraft role predominates, these batteries constitute an important element in the ground defense plan for the vital rear points they are protecting and are prepared to engage any armoured or other forces which may succeed in penetrating to that depth.

Employment in Forward Areas

Light batteries attached to Army units in forward areas may also operate as a whole, but platoons are usually detached to perform special tasks. On the march, platoons are generally spaced at intervals along the column, or are sited at particularly vulnerable points along the route, such as bridges, or crossroads. Their principal task is to protect the column against attack by low flying aircraft; their secondary task is to engage ground forces.

In battle light flak units afford protection for headquarters, field artillery concentrations, infantry concentrations, engineer units, motor parks, and so on. Also, it is sometimes considered necessary to assign a light platoon of three guns to a heavy flak battery engaged in anti-tank work, presumably because, under certain circumstances, the two light guns belonging to the two batteries do not afford enough protection. In all these tasks the anti-aircraft role predominates, but engagement of personnel and armoured vehicles is also regarded as highly important and often takes place. Experience has shown that during tank attacks, light guns, as well as heavy guns, have ignored air targets and have concentrated on hostile armoured vehicles, leaving German ground units to defend themselves against air attack by means of rifle and light machine-gun fire. As previous issues of the Intelligence Bulletin have explained, German Army training stresses the importance of small-arms fire in defense against low-flying aircraft.

NOTE: This section has dealt solely with German Air Force flak. There are also (1) Army flak (Heeresflak) units, which include "mixed" battalions (containing both heavy and light batteries) as part of the artillery, and (2) light companies (Flak), which have light guns only, as part of the infantry. These other types are not numerous, however. As a rule, they are GHQ troops, and are attached to army units in much the same way that German Air Force flak units are attached. Recent enemy documents show that an Army flak battalion, consisting of two heavy batteries and one light battery, is now included in the tables of organization of armoured and motorized divisions.

The problem for both sides was how to effectively defend against an air raid and keep the civilian population safe. The chances of an anti-aircraft battery being able to shoot down enough enemy aircraft, before they dropped their payload of heavy bombs, were slim to say the least.

The following was taken from the edition of the bulletin dated 10 June 1944. Although it does not concern a German anti-aircraft unit, but rather an anti-tank pillbox in Italy, it does describe what the men deployed in such a defensive position had to endure during a raid.

This is interesting as usually such events were only described from an Allied perspective. Knowing how such an attack was viewed by an enemy was useful as it allowed such tactics and operations to be changed and altered for the better if such a need arose.

A German's reaction to a British night attack

After a recent action near Minturno, Italy, in which a British raiding party attacked a German anti-tank-gun pillbox, a German prisoner gave a detailed description of the attack, from an enemy point of view:

> *In the evening of 30 December, the prisoner arrived at the pillbox, which was situated at one end of a bridge across the Garigliano River. He was to serve as the new gun commander. The man already in command, who was to be relieved with his crew the following day, was to give him full instructions as to*

the mission, the targets, and so on. Thus there were two gun commanders in the pillbox at the same time, as well as three crew members. The prisoner stated that a new gun commander had also been dispatched to a second anti-tank gun position, further south, to take over the following day.

At about 2200 hours, the British laid down an artillery barrage. The prisoner commented that although the concrete pillbox received several hits, which shook the occupants severely, it did not collapse. For this reason, he said, he felt comparatively safe; but he admitted that the barrage frayed his nerves badly. He said that he did not blame the German infantry in exposed positions along the west bank of the river for having withdrawn to the rear. However, he added, if these German troops had not withdrawn, it would have been impossible for the British to advance from that direction and, in a surprise move, arrive in his sector.

When the barrage lifted, intense firing was going on east of the river. From the noise and the length of combat, he deduced that the British forward platoon was fighting well.

At about 0400 his entire sector was illuminated by flares. In the bright light he could see some men running in and out of the ruins of a Roman amphitheatre about 200 yards away. He was unable to tell whether they were friend or foe. By this time the men in the pillbox had been joined by a corporal of engineers, who had fled from his post at the river, where he had been on ferrying duty with a small detachment.

During the entire night, frantic discussions went on in the pillbox as to what course of action should be taken; however, since everyone was both confused and frightened, the discussions resulted in nothing more than excited talking and gesturing.

From the entrance, the prisoner suddenly noticed a number of men, about 100 he estimated, rising from the grass to the south and advancing quickly toward the ruins of the amphitheatre. This advance was conducted quite silently, compared to the sounds which came from the amphitheatre a few minutes later. The prisoner said that what happened next was like a fantastic play, with black figures moving in all directions under flares, with the sound of firing mingled with the music of bagpipes. The prisoner said that during lulls in the firing he could observe British troops moving along the main road silently, because of their rubber soles. He observed that this was in marked contrast to the sound of German boots he had heard when, before the attack, German soldiers had been moving about in the vicinity of the amphitheatre.

A number of British soldiers advanced toward the pillbox, and the occupants went into a huddle to try to figure out a means of escape. The prisoner unblocked one of the two apertures, but could barely push his head through. The old gun commander decided to open fire with a machine pistol. He loaded it, fired a magazine, and then shouted for more ammunition, not realizing that five magazines were lying close beside him. The prisoner mustered courage, and fired two rounds with his own machine pistol, only to find that the feeding had stopped, probably because of a broken magazine spring.

Knowing a British attack on their position was imminent, but not knowing what it was going to involve, must have been beyond frightening. Would grenades be thrown inside their stronghold, or a flame thrower unleashed into their midst? At such a time, how does a man even think straight let alone hold himself together in any kind of coherent manner.

The advancing British fired a machine-gun burst into the pillbox, killing the old gun commander and one of the crew. Going to the anti-tank-gun aperture, the prisoner saw some British soldiers moving toward the shelter from the undefended side. The prisoner crouched by the aperture, which had been cleared in the hope that escape in that direction would be possible; however, any such move now was out of the question. A British soldier approached and fired his machine gun into the pillbox. In the dark he unwittingly rested his gun on the prisoner's thigh. The German, who was terrified, remained motionless.

By this time the men in the shelter were so confused that when a smoke hand grenade was hurled through an aperture, they quickly obeyed an order to surrender.

How fortunate for the prisoner and his colleagues that it was only a smoke grenade that had been thrown into their pill box and not an explosive one. It is no wonder they so readily surrendered, shocked to discover they were all still actually alive.

The Germans were led to the amphitheatre and then to the river. They had to swim across the river "a hazardous venture," the prisoner remarked, "because of whirlpools created by the debris of the demolished bridges."

By the time they had reached the other side of the river, German artillery had opened up. The prisoner noticed that during the German artillery fire, British soldiers always hit the ground, whereas the German prisoners remained standing. This prisoner implied that long experience on the receiving end of artillery fire had taught the Germans to judge direction of fire and impact.

"The sureness of the execution and the fact that picked men were employed for the task made the raid a success," the prisoner commented. *He spoke with respect of the use of rubber soles, daggers, blackened faces, and so on, and of the fire power of the light automatic weapons. He said that he felt obliged to couple with these factors the inadequacy of the German defense of the sector. The positions were too far forward, a central command was lacking, and no minefields had been prepared. Before the British attack, he said, he and the other men in the pillbox had discussed "the ridiculous defense layout."*

The prisoner was clearly an intelligent individual who picked up on the smallest of details, down to the fact that the British soldiers had worn rubber soled boots rather than the hob nailed ones worn by his comrades.

CHAPTER 5

Raid on Regensburg and Schweinfurt – 17 August 1943

The city of Schweinfurt, located on the Main River in northern Bavaria, was an important centre of the German war effort. It was in this industrialised city of some 52,000 people where Nazi Germany carried out the manufacture of anti-friction bearings, which were essential in the production of mechanised equipment. The bearings hold or guide moving machine parts, which in turn helps reduce friction and wear, and with the large quantities of artillery guns, vehicles of all descriptions, submarines, ships, and aircraft, they were in massive demand.

Allied intelligence indicated that somewhere in the region of half of all German ball bearing manufacture took place in Schweinfurt, which made it a legitimate military target in the eyes of American and British authorities. The five factories where the ball bearing production was carried out were to be found on the west side of the city. The Allies believed that if they could carry out effective air strikes on these factories, putting them out of action in the process, then it would have a major effect on the German war effort, which in turn could ultimately shorten the war and mean tens of thousands of Allied lives would be saved.

German authorities also knew the importance that Schweinfurt played in the Nazi war effort, resulting in a ring of Flak batteries being put in place around the city.

The specific industrial areas in Schweinfurt that housed the factories where the ball-bearings were made, were heavily protected by anti-aircraft gun and searchlight batteries set up in such a way that they afforded protection against air attacks from any direction. Allied aircraft carrying out raids on the city's industrial area usually approached from the southwest as this provided them with the most direct bombing run to their intended targets. As if to emphasise the city's importance to Nazi Germany, by the end of the war, 140 flak guns had been placed in defensive positions around Schweinfurt, including the infamous 88mm Flak guns, which were both feared and respected in equal amounts by the Allies.

The Germans had given some thought to the type of guns which they deployed in the defensive positions at Schweinfurt. They even had a number of 10.5cm guns, which they used in a mobile capacity by having them mounted on the chassis of railway carriages. Along with the 88mm guns, they specifically targeted the Allied bombers which flew at higher altitudes. The Allied fighters and bombers, both of which flew at a much lower altitude, were targeted by the smaller flak weapons, which were predominantly the 2cm and 3.7cm guns. Mixed in amongst the anti-aircraft batteries were a number of searchlight units which enabled the identification and position of incoming Allied aircraft, which in the main were American, such as the B-17 Flying Fortresses.

Despite all this weaponry, anti-aircraft batteries were always at a disadvantage in comparison to their attackers, although being a crew member of one of the aircraft that were being fired at, was not for the faint hearted.

On the evening of 17 August 1943, an Allied raid involving both American and British aircraft carried out an operation that was intended to conduct air raids on both Schweinfurt and Regensburg. The operation, known as Mission No.84, involved 376 B-17 Flying Fortresses, four engine heavy bomber aircraft of the United States Eighth Air Force, along with a number of American P-47 Thunderbolt fighter aircraft, which could also be utilised in a fighter-bomber ground attack role with the addition of 5-inch rockets. RAF Spitfires were also part of the operation.

The Regensburg aspect of the mission involved 146 B-17s, consisting of seven groups, six of which were flying in a 21-aircraft 'combat box tactical formation', with the seventh consisting of 20 aircraft. These seven groups were organised in three larger formations, known as 'provisional combat wings', each of which flew in a 'V' formation, with the group at the rear flying at a lower altitude.

Because of human error, not all of the fighter aircraft that had been tasked with escorting the bombers to the

German border arrived at the designated rendezvous point on time, meaning that the American bombers were extremely vulnerable to attack by German fighters. The Luftwaffe had some 400 fighter aircraft in the skies at the peak of the raid, but after an hour and a half they had to break off, low on both fuel and ammunition. During the attack they had managed to bring down 15 of the American bombers, but this still left 131 B-17 Flying Fortresses to drop their bombs on Regensburg, targeting the German aircraft factories. By the time the raid was over, the Americans had dropped a mind boggling 298.75 tons of bombs on the city, made somewhat easier because of clear skies and light anti-aircraft defences. But even if there had been maximum anti-aircraft coverage, just how effective could it have been against such a large number of enemy aircraft?

Having completed their mission, the surviving B-17s that had made the 600 mile journey to Regensburg, deep into southern Germany, made their way south. Two of the aircraft landed in Switzerland where their crews were interned and the planes confiscated. Colonel LeMay, the man in charge of the raid on Regensburg, then set a course for Tunisia, some 1,300 miles away. En route one of the aircraft had to crash land in Italy, whilst a further five landed in the Mediterranean Sea having run out of fuel. In total, 122 of the B-17 heavy bombers made it to Tunisia in North Africa, with more than half of them having sustained significant damage from a combination of attacks from German fighters and the ground-based anti-aircraft units deployed around the city of Regensburg.

Although the mission inflicted a great deal of damage on the targets at Regensburg, it came at a price: 60 Flying Fortresses were lost, with a further 95 damaged, many beyond repair.

As the aircraft which had attacked Regensburg, made good their escape, the 230 American aircraft that had been allocated to attack the German city of Schweinfurt had already taken off from their respective airfields in southern England, and formed in the skies over East Anglia in twelve groups stretched over a distance of some 20 miles. The task force of planes that headed for Schweinfurt flew the same route as those who had flown to Regensburg before them. The 230 B-17s were escorted by eight squadrons, or 96 RAF Spitfires, as far as Antwerp, where they handed over their escort duties to a group of American P-47s. Orders for the mission stated that the B-17s should fly at an altitude of between 23,000 and 26,500 feet, but as they approached the Dutch coastline they were confronted by a massive cloud base which had not been anticipated. The decision was taken to fly underneath the clouds as the task force commander, Brigadier-General Robert B. Williams, a co-pilot on one of the leading aircraft, did not believe that his aircraft would be able to climb above the clouds. The main problem with this was that by flying under the cloud, which was at 17,000 feet, they had made themselves vulnerable, not only to German aircraft but also to anti-aircraft batteries.

A large number of aircraft of the Luftwaffe lay in wait, including Messerschmitt Bf 109s and Focke-Wulf Fw 190s. The initial part of the aerial battle began before the Spitfires handed over their escort duties, but before doing so, they accounted for eight of the German fighters. There was a problem with the handover of the escort for the B-17s, because for some reason the Spitfires didn't wait to make a visual hand over to their American counterparts, but instead broke off at the agreed rendezvous point. The American P-47 fighters arrived between five and eight minutes late.

Once the raiding party entered German airspace, the number of their aircraft that entered the affray increased dramatically to more than 300. At 2.30pm, an hour after having first crossed the Dutch border, and upon reaching the German city of Worms on the Upper Rhine, the B-17s suddenly changed direction and began heading northeast. Prior to this it would not have been clear what or where their intended target was. Now the German defenders knew that their destination was Schweinfurt, but at a distance of 140 miles, they only had approximately half an hour to shoot down as many of the bombers as possible.

The anti-aircraft batteries in and around Schweinfurt were immediately put on full alert for the imminent raid that was coming their way. In the meantime, the German fighters did their best and managed to shoot down 22 of the American B-17 heavy bombers. But just 15 miles out from Schweinfurt, the German fighters had to disengage to return to their bases to refuel and re-arm as quickly as they could, so that they were ready and waiting for the American aircraft as they made their return journey.

When the bomber force was just 5 miles from Schweinfurt, the anti-aircraft guns opened fire. They were not actually aiming at a direct target but laying out a flak barrage in front of the B-17s that the Germans hoped they would fly directly into. The raid on Schweinfurt began just before 3pm, but by then the 57 bombers of the lead wing carrying out the attack had already been reduced to 40. Within just twenty-four minutes the 143 aircraft of the other two wings of the raiding party had entered the affray as well. During that relatively short period of time the combined force of 183 bombers dropped 424 tons of bombs, which included 125 tons of incendiaries, but any kind of accuracy became more difficult with each bomb that was dropped because of the resulting heavy plumes of smoke.

The anti-aircraft guns had some success as they managed to shoot down three of the B-17 bombers, which may have been good luck rather than accurate firing. If the bombers couldn't see their intended targets, then the chances are the anti-aircraft batteries could not see the American aircraft that they knew were in the skies above them. But the noise of their engines would have been a strong indicator as to where they were. The rapid and repetitive fire of the anti-aircraft batteries was bound to prove successful eventually, just because of the number of rounds that they fired. By the time the Schweinfurt raid was over, the Americans had lost 36 of their B-17 bombers.

As a result of the double targeted mission on 17 August 1943, the Americans initially listed a total of 552 of their crewmen missing in action, although subsequent to that information it came to light that around half of that number had in fact been captured by the Germans and became prisoners of war, with another twenty interned in Switzerland. Of the aircraft that returned to the UK after the mission, 7 of those crewmen were dead with a further 21 wounded.

How effective were the German anti-aircraft batteries in both Regensburg and Schweinfurt? It is a difficult question to answer fairly because the two raids were not exactly the same when it came to the weather conditions, the number of defending aircraft, the number of attacking aircraft and the number of anti-aircraft units based at both locations. But none of these varying factors can ultimately change the results and impact of either of the raids. A point worth mentioning with facts and figures and how varied they can be, is highlighted with this particular mission, in that their accuracy comes down to the honesty of those who provided the figures. If the claims of the gunners on board the B-17 Flying Fortresses were to be believed, then they shot down a total of 288 German fighters, whilst Luftwaffe records record only 27 of their aircraft were lost. Just how different is it possible for such figures to be?

In Regensburg, where Messerschmitt aircraft were manufactured, the six main workshops where the aircraft were built and assembled were all destroyed or heavily damaged as a result of the raid. As for Schweinfurt, although the overall damage was extensive, it was less than had been caused at Regensburg. All of the cities' four ball bearing factories were damaged, with at least part of each of them being destroyed. Nearly all of the factories sustained extensive fire damage as a result of the incendiaries. This resulted in much of the machinery used in the factories sustaining fire damage, due to the machine oil that was part of the manufacturing process igniting.

The Kugelfischer-Georg-Schäfer factory, which was the largest of the four, was located north of the city's main railway sidings, and employed 11,700 paid employees along with a number of slave labourers. The Vereinigte Kugellagerfabriken AG company consisted of two factories, the first in the centre of the city with the other to the south of the railway yards. Collectively, these factories were struck by eighty direct hits from the American bombers, although the Kugelfischer factory was the only one which did not sustain any extensive fire damage. The Fichtel & Sachs factory was situated south of the railway yards and owned by a Swedish company. The last of the factories, owned by the Deutsche Star GmbH company, was also on the southern side of the railway yards.

A total of 203 civilians were killed during the raid, many of whom were workers in the factories that were bombed.

How did the men who served with the anti-aircraft batteries feel in the immediate aftermath of a raid which had been carried out on a factory, town or city that they were deployed to defend? Did they focus on how many enemy aircraft they had managed to shoot down, or was the measure of how successful they had, or had not been, based on the level of damage that had been caused and the number of people who had been killed? An interesting thought to also consider is how the people of a town or city felt towards the men of these same batteries, after their communities and homes had been devastated by such raids.

Being a member of an anti-aircraft battery must have been a thankless task to some degree, because no matter how hard the men tried, or how fast they managed to fire their guns, they knew that they were never going to be able to prevent enemy aircraft from dropping their bombs on the locations they were defending. Once the bombing began they couldn't run off to the nearest air raid shelter and sit it out until the all clear was sounded, but had to stay with their battery no matter how dangerous things became.

Second Schweinfurt Raid – 14 October 1943

Despite the effectiveness of the August attack on Schweinfurt, the Allies had decided another such raid on the city was required to once again damage and destroy the factories where Germany was producing a large quantity of her ball bearings required for the war effort.

The raid in August had initially reduced Germany's ball bearing production by 34 per cent, but the cost had been high in both aircraft and men. The number of aircraft lost on that first raid had been so great that a planned second raid was cancelled to allow time for more aircraft to be built. Lessons had been learnt from the first raid that would hopefully make the second raid even more successful in reducing ball bearing production.

The second raid was carried out by aircraft of the USAAF. Out of the 291 B-17 Flying Fortresses sent on that raid, 60 were lost, 17 were so badly damaged that they had to be scrapped, with a further 121 that returned with noticeable damage. Of the 2,900 aircrew who took part in the raid, 650 of them lost their lives, which equates to 22 per cent of the bomber crews.

The other important lesson that had been learnt was in relation to the provision of fighter escorts, although despite ensuring that they had what they believed was sufficient cover, it clearly didn't prevent them from sustaining heavy losses.

Third Schweinfurt Raid – 24 February 1944

The fact that there had to be a third raid on the ball bearing factories at Schweinfurt was down to a combination of a stout German defence, coupled with a strong need and determination to get ball bearing manufacture back as quickly as possible, added to the Allied inability to carry out an effective bombing of the city's industrial area.

On the evening of 24 February 1944, more than 1,000 aircraft of the RAF left air bases across the UK and made their way to Germany. A total of 734 Lancaster, Halifax and Mosquito bombers took off from stations such as RAF Warboys in Cambridgeshire, which was one of the original Pathfinder Force airfields. The building of RAF Warboys had begun in 1940, specifically to relieve the congestion at RAF Upwood for the use of No.17 Operational Training Unit.

The other 300 aircraft did not take part in the actual raid on Schweinfurt, but were deployed as either support aircraft, or on diversionary raids to keep the Germans uncertain for as long as possible as to where the main target of the raid was going to be.

Because of the importance of the ball bearing factories at Schweinfurt, it was an area that was extremely well protected, with a number of anti-aircraft batteries set up not just to protect the factories themselves, but the aerial routes that would be taken by the American aircraft as they made their way to their intended targets. There were fourteen in total, the locations of which are listed below. The main weapon for each of the batteries was the 88mm Flak Gun.

Bergrheinfeld	Deutschohof	Ettleben	Euerbach
Geldersheim	Grafenrheinfeld	Grossbatterie	Hambach
Kaltenhof	Oberndorf	Rothlein	Schwebheim
Sennfeld/ Gochsheim	Spitalholz		

Between these batteries a total of 175 88mm guns were in place to defend the ball bearing factories at Schweinfurt. Three of the sites each had six guns; seven of the sites had twelve; three had eighteen guns, and one site had nineteen. However, not all of the batteries were necessarily operational at the same time. There was fluidity in how these batteries were used, such that at any given time they may well have had more or less of the guns in operation at each of their locations. There were also four mobile batteries which used 105mm guns and were kept on flattened rail cars so that they could be moved from place to place at a moment's notice. The starting point for each of these batteries was near

Bergrheinfeld railway station, Gochsheim, Kugelfischer and Niederwerrn.

With somewhere in the region of 200 of these big guns in use, and with each one requiring about eight men to operate them and keep them firing to an effective level, a minimum of 1,600 men were required to man all of these batteries.

Although flying out of British RAF bases, this was an American idea and operation carried out by B-17 Flying Fortresses of the USAAF. This was an operation that the Air Officer Commanding-in-Chief of RAF Bomber Command, Arthur 'Bomber' Harris, did not agree with and refused to support. He actually went as far as to question the military intelligence which had led to the Americans to come up with a plan to conduct a raid on Schweinfurt in the first place. Harris did not believe that there was any need to attack the factories which made ball bearings, and that any such raids would not significantly damage the German war effort or affect her ability to continue to produce large quantities of war machines for land, air or sea. His doubts were subsequently proven to be correct when post war analysis showed that Nazi Germany had spent the years before the war building up massive stocks of ball bearings, having brought in supplies from countries all over Europe, including the war time neutral countries of Sweden and Switzerland.

The area of Schweinfurt had been identified as early as 1942 as being a significant centre for ball bearing production in Germany, with 43 per cent of her war time needs being manufactured there. This in turn then made it an identified

Allied, and particularly an American, target. Even if the two big air raids carried out on Schweinfurt by the Americans had been successful enough to totally obliterate the factories producing the ball bearings, it would have had little if no effect because of the reserves that Germany had amassed before the war began.

During the Second World War, Schweinfurt was attacked by American and British bomber aircraft on twenty-two separate occasions, dropping a total of 7,933 tons of bombs in the process. Production in the city's four ball bearing factories continued throughout the war, until it eventually came to an end on 11 April 1945 when the city was captured by elements of the United States 42nd Infantry Division.

CHAPTER 6

Combined Bomber Offensive

Such targets as the ball bearing factory at Schweinfurt were usually identified by the Combined Bomber Offensive, a joint American and British offensive for the strategic bombing of targets throughout Europe, but mainly in Germany. These operations reached their peak between June 1943 and May 1944. Their main targets usually concerned installations, factories and plants involved in the manufacture of petroleum, oil, and lubrication for the German war effort. Their nominated targets included railway sidings, rail tracks and other transportation targets.

The existence of the Allied Combined Bomber Offensive was a major problem for Hitler's air defences, both the anti-aircraft batteries and their own fighter aircraft that were used to attack British and American bombers carrying out missions on targets throughout Germany.

Operation Pointblank was the code name given to the primary thrust of the Allied Combined Bomber Offensive, which was to eliminate the effectiveness of Germany's fighter aircraft strength, and in doing so draw them away from frontline operations. The ultimate goal was to stop or greatly reduce their air superiority by the time of the intended Allied invasion of Nazi-occupied Europe in June 1944.

The operation had two aspects to it. The bombing raids on targets throughout Germany not only tied up large numbers of her fighter aircraft and provided the opportunity to destroy many of them in the air, but many of the targets that Allied bombers attacked were either aircraft factories or factories that manufactured vital parts that were needed in their construction process.

The Pointblank directive, dated 14 June 1943, could be classed as a game changer as far as the Allies were concerned, because prior to this the Royal Air Force and the United States Army Air Force were basically doing their own thing. The British were engaged in nighttime missions and usually targeted large industrial areas that were used in the manufacture of items for Germany's war effort, whereas the American aircraft were deployed on daytime operations against specific identified targets. From a German perspective this was a nightmare scenario, as it meant that their anti-aircraft batteries and fighter aircraft were on the go twenty-four hours a day, giving them little or no respite.

Here are just some of the war time industries that the anti-aircraft batteries and fighter aircraft of the Luftwaffe had to try to defend against the ever-increasing number of air raids carried out by American and British bombers.

- Ball bearing factories.
- Petroleum, oil and lubrication factories.

- Factories involved in the production of 'grinding wheels' and 'crude abrasives'.
- Premises used for the manufacture of synthetic rubber and rubber tyres.
- Submarine construction works and bases.
- Plants or factories where military vehicles used for transport were manufactured.
- A coking plant: an oil refinery processing unit which converts residue oil from the vacuum distillation column into low molecular weight hydrocarbon gases, light and heavy gas oils, and petroleum coke.
- Iron and steel works.
- Factories that produced machine tools.
- Electric power stations.
- Anywhere that electrical war related electrical equipment was manufactured.
- Factories that manufactured optical precision equipment.
- Chemical plants.
- Plants where nitrogen was produced.

Most major cities had some kind of anti-aircraft cover, if for no other reason than to provide an acceptable level of reassurance to the civilian population. All the Allies had to do was to send their aircraft to take photographs of Germany, and anywhere they discovered a large concentration of anti-aircraft batteries, there was more than likely to be some kind of factory, installation, works, base or station, which had a military use, purpose or connection, making it a justifiable target. The Allies then had to discover what it was these anti-aircraft batteries were in place to protect, and then determine whether there was a need to send their bombers to destroy it.

The German 88cm Flak gun was first and foremost an anti-aircraft gun, but it was also an anti-tank weapon as well. It was once described by an un-named British Army officer serving in North Africa as not only being an anti-aircraft gun but as being, 'unfair and anti-everything'. It was without doubt one of the best, if not the best, weapon that Germany had in her military arsenal throughout the Second World War. Early on in the war the Germans quickly discovered that it wasn't just an anti-aircraft weapon, but also a very useful weapon against tanks and fortified bunkers. This was because of its stretched trajectory, high muzzle velocity and deep penetration ability. It was also used as a quick firing artillery gun, with which a well-trained crew could fire up to twenty rounds a minute over a protracted period, in whatever mode of firing it was being used.

Different versions of the 88cm gun were adapted for use on German naval vessels as well as submarines, or as a mobile flak battery on a train. One of its downsides was its size and weight, which meant it was more readily spotted by Allied aircraft and harder to move quickly. Its open design meant that the crew needed to operate it were afforded no protection whatsoever.

Another of the German anti-aircraft weapons feared by Allied pilots was the 2cm *Flakvierling*, or quadruple flak gun, which had devastating fire power. It had multi-purpose use, either as a stationary weapon on the rear of a half-tracked vehicle, a Panzer IV chassis, or on ships or trains.

Besides these two weapons the Germans developed even larger and more powerful anti-aircraft weapons, such as the 10.5cm and the 12.8cm flak guns. The 10.5 Flak gun was capable of firing up to fifteen rounds per minute – or one every four seconds – up to a height of 31,000 feet, with its bigger brother, the 12.8cm gun, able to fire up to ten rounds per minute – or one every six seconds – up to 35,000 feet, which is higher than altitude of one of today's commercial aircrafts. During the war there was continuous production of both of these weapons, with 4,200 10.5cm flak guns being manufactured, and 1,128 12.8cm flak guns. These included thirty-three twin flak guns, which were place on top of the Flak towers in Berlin, Hamburg and Vienna.

Despite its fearsome reputation, it has been estimated that, on average, an 88cm Flak gun needed to fire somewhere in the region of 15,000 rounds to bring down just one Allied heavy bomber. With a capability of firing twenty rounds a minute, that means it would take twelve and a half hours of constant firing for an 88 to bring down just one Allied aircraft. As for the 10.5cm Flak gun, an average number of rounds it would have to fire to be able to do the same was estimated to be 6,000 rounds, whilst the 12.8cm Flak gun only needed 3,000 rounds.

CHAPTER 7

German Searchlight Units

The searchlights which Germany used throughout the Second World War as part of her anti-aircraft batteries only began to be developed in 1927. This was directly connected to Germany's signing of the Treaty of Versailles at the end of the First World War which forbade the developing of such equipment.

At the outbreak of war in 1939, Germany's searchlights were used in conjunction with acoustic direction finders, which by the end of the war had been replaced and upgraded to being radar directed. In both cases the powerful searchlights, which used extremely high-powered carbon arc lamps, were guided to the right area of the skies, where they swept back and forth until they found the target they were looking for, which in most cases meant American or British aircraft.

The first carbon arc searchlight had actually been built in America in 1893. It was made by the General Electric company and first appeared at the World's Columbian exposition of 1893, in Chicago.

During the Second World War Germany used three different sizes of searchlight, the 60cm, the 150cm and the 200cm.

The following information is taken from a United States War Department Publication compiled by their Military Intelligence Service, and dated February 1943. This only applies to the 60cm and 150cm guns as the 200cm version did not come into service until later in the year, although the report does make mention of its 'recent development'.

The 60 Centimetre Searchlight

The 60cm, or 24-inch diameter parabolic glass reflector, which in essence was the searchlight, was powered by an 8 kilowatt generator. The light output of the searchlight was rated at 135 million candelas, which in layman's terms meant that it generated an extremely bright light, giving it an effective detection range of just over 3 miles. (For comparison a common wax candle emits light with a luminous intensity of roughly one candela.) As impressive as that sounds, these searchlights could only reach as high as 4,900 feet, which meant that Allied aircraft would have to be flying at a relatively low altitude before they could be picked up. Because of their inability to reach the heights at which Allied bombers flew, they were usually deployed alongside 20mm and 37mm, low level ceiling flak guns.

If the beam of the searchlight was dispersed its detection rate was reduced to just two miles, which greatly impaired its effectiveness. Each searchlight was transportable on a single axle trailer and required a five-man crew including a section commander, searchlight controller, lamp attendant, generator attendant and driver. There was a naval version of this which included shutters, thus allowing it to be used to signal Morse code. To assist the operator the searchlight had two hand-operated manual cranks which were used in the calculation of altitude and distance, and moved from side to side.

This was a well built and truly sophisticated piece of German engineering that was far better than anything that British forces had. The 8-kilowatt generator that powered the searchlight, was itself driven by a six cylinder BMW engine, which before the war had been of the type used to drive BMW cars.

One of the main tactics deployed by the searchlight team was to move their light in an S-shaped movement along the expected flight path of the Allied aircraft, with the beam in the dispersed mode once a target aircraft had been discovered. Once this had occurred the searchlight was switched back to being used by the fully focused beam.

The 150 Centimetre Searchlight

The 150 centimetre, 34 and 37 *Flakscheinwerfer*, or Flak Searchlight, was developed in the late 1930s, had a detection range of about 5 miles and were effective at locating and identifying Allied aircraft at an altitude of up to about 16,000 feet.

The searchlight's 59-inch diameter parabolic glass reflectors, had an output of 990 million candelas, making it an extremely useful piece of equipment. It was powered by a 24-kilowatt generator, which was three times the size of the generator in use with the 60-centimetre searchlight, and it required a 51 horsepower, 8-cylinder engine.

The 150-centimetre searchlight could be traversed 360 degrees and elevated from −12 degrees, through the vertical to −12 degrees on the opposite side. Because of its size, when moved between locations, it required two trailers, one for the actual searchlight and one for the generator. It needed a fourteen-man crew to operate it including section commander, searchlight layer for elevation, searchlight controller and layer for azimuth, lamp attendant, optical director spotter, general attendant, engine attendant, lag-calculator operator, azimuth listener, elevation listener, sound locator spotter and three drivers.

Tactics with its deployment early in the war had it placed in front of the Flak guns in what the Germans called a 'zone of preparation'. This saw them set out in a grid formation about 3 miles apart. Like their smaller 'cousin', the 60-centimetre searchlight, they were initially assisted by sound locators and then radar systems, to help them locate Allied aircraft.

Always looking to improve on what they had, the Germans looked to increase the range of the 150-centimetre searchlights. To this end they came up with the idea of making quadruple 150-centimetre mounts, of which they manufactured sixty-one, but these proved to be unsuccessful, hence why such a small number of them were made, and they were never mass produced.

The 200-Centimetre Searchlights

The largest of Germany's wartime searchlights was the 200 centimetre, Scheinwerfer-43 searchlight, but these didn't come on-line until 1943, five years into the war; this was still enough time for 2,262 of them to be manufactured and brought into service. The reason for its introduction was that many of the Allied bombers carrying out air raids over Germany were doing so at much higher levels of altitude than they had been during the early years of the war. This was because they had learned a costly lesson in the losses they had sustained by flying at lower altitudes, both in the number of aircraft they had lost and had damaged, many of which had then been beyond repair, along with the number of air crew casualties.

Each of these improved and more powerful searchlights emitted 2.7 billion Hefner candlepower, which were powered by a 120-kilowatt generator, which was nearly five times bigger than the generators which powered the 150-centimetre searchlights.

The main difference with the 200-centimetre searchlight was twofold: firstly, it could pick out an Allied aircraft when it was over 8 miles away from its intended target, and secondly, it was rarely deployed on its own. Instead, it was used as the central and main searchlight, surrounded by three of the smaller and less powerful 150-centimetre searchlights. Collectively the four searchlights would locate and entrap an Allied aircraft, providing a clear and precise target for the Flak guns to aim at.

A point worth noting in relation to the smaller searchlights of 60 and 150 centimetres, was that in September 1940, at a time when the German homeland had yet to experience large scale Allied bombing raids, German forces had a total of 2,540 of these searchlights. By February 1944, this number had increased dramatically to 13,687.

The 60-centimetre searchlight was usually deployed in conjunction with light Flak batteries or gun platoons, meaning that any communications needed to make were done via these units.

An interesting aspect of all of these searchlights is that none of them were designed or built with the safety or wellbeing of the crews who would have to operate them. They offered absolutely no protection from any incoming enemy fire, possibly because it was not expected that they would come under attack from any Allied aircraft. The only protection which they could have had, was if they were deployed in some kind of defensive position which saw them partly below ground level or incorporated within a position which had raised sides. Why they had no armoured shields to at least protect them from incoming enemy machine gun fire, is unclear.

When the searchlights and their generators were not in use, many of them were placed inside bunkers or other similar structures. This not only helped to keep them safe from daytime bombing raids but also acted as a maintenance garage where any repair work that was required could be carried out. It also acted as accommodation for the searchlight crews.

A number of these searchlights, especially the 60-centimetre version, survived the war and are today either kept in museums or as part of private collections.

CHAPTER 8

German Barrage Balloons

Barrage Balloons were very large gas-filled balloons, some 60 feet in length and more than 20 feet in diameter, which were tethered to the ground, or the deck of a ship, by metal cables and were a defence against low altitude air raids. They were used extensively by both sides throughout the war and were effective in two main ways. Their presence made life extremely difficult for any enemy aircraft trying to fly to its target at a low altitude, as these aircraft ran the risk of either crashing into the balloons or the cables that connected them to the ground.

Their main purpose was to protect a city's buildings and population, along with military targets, such as ports, factories, airfields, dockyards and military establishments. They forced attacking aircraft to fly at an altitude above 5,000 feet, which helped hinder the accuracy of their bombing. There was an obvious disadvantage to barrage balloons as their very presence was a clear indication to enemy aircraft that the ground beneath them had areas that were worth bombing. Barrage balloons served no other

Right: The Luftwaffe Flak Badge was awarded to servicemen of the Flak artillery who distinguished themselves in action against enemy aerial or ground attacks.

Below: German 88mm guns being deployed on a Marinefährprahm (MFP) "naval ferry barge"; the largest landing craft operated by Germany's Kriegsmarine during the Second World War.

A German Shepherd dog dressed up to look like an aircraft spotter by his 88mm anti-aircraft gun crew.

Two brand new German 2cm Flak 38 guns on what appears to be a parade square, possibly during a course on how to use them.

Above: A German 128mm flak gun ready for action on a Flak tower in the Tiergarten, Berlin 1945.

Below: Four German Flak 88mm anti-aircraft guns and their crews.

Above: The crew of an 88mm gun trying to shoot down Allied aircraft during an air raid.

Left: A German naval anti-aircraft gunner, without any kind of ballistic cover shield, trying to bring down an Allied aircraft.

Above: German 88mm guns on train carriages allowing them to be used in a mobile capacity. The soldiers in the foreground wearing shorts and no shirt suggest that the photograph was taken in the summer months.

Right: A German 85cm Flak 41 gun located in a fortified coastal position, with one of the gun crew looking through his binoculars for any potential Allied aerial threat.

The five-man crew of a German 2cm Flak gun preparing to take on Allied aircraft. This was a weapon that was capable of firing 220 rounds per minute and was a vast improvement on the previous version, which only had a firing rate of 120 rounds per minute. At the beginning of the war, the 2cm Flak 38 was being use by both the Wehrmacht and the Kriegsmarine.

A German observer searches the skies for a target, whilst the rest of the gun crew prepare to fire their camouflaged four barrelled anti-aircraft gun.

Above: A burnt out 37mm gun on the rear of a converted Hanomag Sd Kfz. 11. A German military priest stands by its side, possibly saying a prayer for those who were killed.

Below: A German soldier manoeuvres his 38 Flak gun whilst on the lookout for any incoming Allied aircraft. Note the other German soldier in the background, who appears to be acting as an additional lookout.

Above: A unit of Luftwaffe anti-aircraft gunners pose in front of their 88mm gun, situated on top of a Flak tower.

Below: A German 38 Flak gun being readied by its crew. Reliable and effective throughout the war, its four 20mm auto-cannons would have provided real destructive fire power, and could destroy any aircraft it hit fairly quickly.

Above: A seven-man Kriegsmarine unit ready their 20mm anti-aircraft gun as they search the skies for a target.

Right: The crew of a German 88mm anti-aircraft gun being readied for use during a night air raid. The 88mm gun could propel its 20.25-pound high-explosive shell to altitudes beyond 30,000 feet at a rate of about 15 shells per minute.

Left: The crew of a German 88mm anti-aircraft gun preparing to load it ready for firing at enemy aircraft. Notice the German soldiers holding the shells with the tips pointing downwards as the soldier in the middle of the image inserts one into a tube. The high-explosive shells had a yellow coloured tip to them, while the fuse was in the very tip of the shell.

Below: Three German 88mm anti-aircraft guns, each of which have the ends of their gun barrels covered. The guns are either being readied for deployment, or are being collected after use before being redeployed to another location.

Above: A painting of a German 38 Flak, single barrelled, 20mm anti-aircraft gun by an unknown artist. It shows a two-man crew: a loader and a firer.

Below: The crew of an 88mm anti-aircraft gun being made ready for deployment. Whilst one soldier appears to be unhooking the weapon from its towing vehicle, the man second from the right is lowering one of the gun's "legs" to the ground. The vehicle registration number, WL – 30471, indicates that the gun was manned by Luftwaffe personnel (WL representing Wehrmacht Luftwaffe).

Four members of a German Flak gun unit enjoying a cigarette break in their gun encampment, albeit looking slightly uncomfortable at having to pose for the photographer. There appears to be a light snow on the ground indicating it was taken during winter months, and there is even a young child with a football in the background.

The crew of a German 4-barrelled 20mm anti-aircraft gun on top of a Flak tower, searching the skies for the arrival of Allied aircraft. Notice what looks to be another Flak tower in the back ground. From 1940 onwards, Berlin had three Flak towers, whilst Hamburg had two, and Stuttgart and Frankfurt had one each. Meanwhile, Vienna had three of these massive towers to help protect its civilian population from Allied air raids.

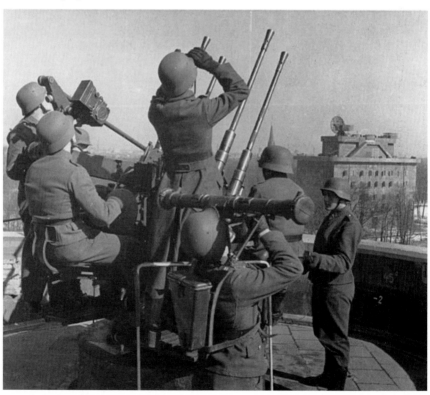

Above: A German Hanomag Sd Kfz. 11 half-track vehicle converted to carry a Flak gun. All of the soldiers are wearing their great coats with their collars up, with one even wearing a balaclava under his cap, suggesting that the photograph was taken during the cold winter months.

Below: A burnt out German half-track vehicle, which looks like it has sustained a direct hit, has been converted to carry a Flak gun. Notice the face of a young man or woman immediately to the right of the destroyed gun, almost ghost-like in its appearance.

British soldiers and an RAF officer examine a German helmet after the Bruneval raid in February 1942. The radio-location receiver at Bruneval was believed to be responsible for the loss of a number of British bomber aircraft and also gave the Germans early warning of any Allied ships and aircraft approaching the coast of Western Europe. Yet despite its importance, it was not heavily defended and had no significant anti-aircraft capability.

A German half-track sdkfz 6.2 adapted to carry a 3.7cm Flak 36 gun and crew in what is clearly a posed photograph. The 3.7cm Flak 18/36/37 were a series of German anti-aircraft guns produced by Nazi Germany, and saw widespread use during the Second World War. The cannon was fully automatic and effective against aircraft flying at altitudes of up to 4,200m.

A German searchlight unit attached to the rear of a vehicle, with its operator sat behind it. The lights came in three main sizes: 60, 150 and 200cm. The one in this image was the smallest of three.

These searchlights appear to be located on the top of a Flak tower, or from the roof of a very tall building, and would be used in conjunction with anti-aircraft units to shoot down any Allied aircraft caught in their stream. The 60cm searchlight had a parabolic glass reflector and was powered by an 8 kilowatt generator. The light output that was generated by this sized light was rated at 135 million candelas, and had a detection range of about 5 kilometres (just over 3 miles) for aircraft travelling at low altitude.

Above: An early model of a German wartime Wurzburg mobile radar. The later versions were much bigger and tended to be of a static nature. Along with anti-aircraft batteries and searchlight units, they insured that Nazi Germany had an effective anti-aircraft capability.

Below: A German four-barrelled Flak 38 anti-aircraft gun and its crew practising their drills. This was the number one German light anti-aircraft gun throughout the war, as well as being their most produced artillery piece of the entire war. Although there were variety of different types, the Flakvierling 38, with its four combined barrels, was the most popular.

purpose than to provide protection for the area underneath which they were deployed.

During the Second World War Germany used barrage balloons not only to protect important sites and locations, but also to protect convoys of military vehicles on the move. The coastal town of Kiel was one such location that was protected by barrage balloons operated by the *Sperrabteilungen*. The Germans also extensively deployed barrage balloons above ports in northern France.

For a nation that had meticulously planned the very moment in time when she was going to put in motion a list of events that would result in the outbreak of the Second World War, Germany had never given much thought to the use of barrage balloons. Perhaps this was because she had never perceived a time that they would be needed to be deployed throughout Germany, although once the war began she wasn't slow in realising the advantages of their use. They provided a feeling of safety for the civil population, whose towns and cities they protected, but fear and trepidation for Allied pilots who were unfortunate enough to fly into an area where they had been deployed. But in fact the Nazi authorities used them not to protect their people, but important buildings and other such nominated locations that were used for manufacturing equipment, ammunition, vehicles, aircraft, ships, and submarines, for the German war effort.

Although it was the barrage balloon itself that was the visible deterrent, especially for Allied pilots, it was actually the steel cable which the balloon was there to hold in place that was the real danger. If a pilot ploughed in to one of these cables he would be lucky to survive. At best it would slice into one of his wings, if not remove it entirely. The chances of being able to parachute to safety from such a low altitude and survive were remote. A lot of thought went into barrage balloons, and they were not just thrown up haphazardly. Detailed engineering information was included in the type of steel used in the cables that were used, including a cable's capacity to resist wind stress.

At the beginning of the Second World War, Germany had two different types of barrage balloon that were used in a military capacity, both of which included four fins, at what was referred to as the tail end. Three of these fins, the top one and the side two, were inflated with air, whilst the bottom fin, which was also known as the 'steering stack', had openings at both ends which once in the deployed allowed air to flow through it and helped keep the balloon in the correct position.

Both types had their main balloon compartment filled with hydrogen gas, but the second and newer of the two also included an amount of air. The main body of the balloon consisted of up to six separate chambers, so that if one was punctured, the balloon did not automatically deflate. The newer type of the two balloons which included air was innovative, in that the higher the balloon travelled, the gas would expand, forcing the air out via valves, when it would then finally come to rest. The largest of these balloons was some 60 feet in length and 25 feet in diameter.

The number of balloons deployed in any one location depended on what they were there to protect, which could also be an indicator as to the importance of what lay beneath them. Seen by an approaching flight of Allied aircraft, German barrage balloons were often incorrectly recorded number wise, in that more often than not the numbers reported were far greater than the actual number present. This was often down to the psychological effect on the bomber crews, as because of the angle and distance from which they were observing, what they were looking at often looked a lot denser than it actually was.

The following is taken from a United States, Military Intelligence Service report dated 10 February 1943:

According to reports, the German barrage balloons usually form an irregular belt about five-eighths of a mile wide and about 1¾ miles from the outer edge of the target area. There is reputedly anywhere between 200 and 800 yards between the balloons. The balloons are flown at varying heights at different times, the exact height and numbers of balloons flown, depends on the time of day, the weather, and the threat of aerial attack.

The purpose of the balloon barrage is to form an irregular pattern of perpendicular steel cables in the vicinity of the defended area, presenting a real as well as a mental hazard to any hostile aviator attempting to fly below the level of the balloons. The net result is to discourage hostile flyers from entering the region of the barrage for dive bombing tactics against the defended area, and to force hostile planes to an altitude less favourable for precision bombing. The plan for a barrage is co-ordinated with light, medium and heavy calibre gun defence, any gaps in the barrage being covered by light and medium Flak. It should be noted that in defending areas which include harbours and docks, the balloon barrage may extend over water, balloons being suspended from stationary or movable barges.

With a Flak shell explosion covering a distance of approximately 200 metres in diameter, there was the obvious danger that any number of balloons could also possibly be destroyed, which in turn could leave an even bigger gap through which Allied bombers could drop their bombs with some degree of accuracy.

CHAPTER 9

Chaff and Electronic Counter Measures

Chaff was an item dropped by attacking aircraft on defensive enemy positions to confuse their radar systems with false echoes. Germany's equivalent of chaff was called *Duppel,* so named because that was the suburb in Berlin where tests on this new invention were first carried out in 1942.

In essence attacking aircraft would drop thin pieces of aluminium, plastic or metallised glass fibre in an effort to swamp defensive radar systems with multiple hits, which would produce the effect that the system must either not be working properly or that large clusters of chaff, deposited close together, were in fact enemy aircraft, when they were not. It had been determined that the ideal size for chaff, or *Duppel*, was 10.63 inches in length by 0.79 of an inch in width, and dropped in bundles weighing one pound.

Part of the German air defences deployed to detect British and American aircraft was the Freya radar system.

Besides having to deal with the problems caused by the dropping of chaff over areas throughout Germany which had been identified by the Allies as legitimate targets, both military and civilian, they also had to contend with Allied airborne jamming devices with such code names as Jostle, Mandrel and Piperjack.

Jostle was an airborne jamming transmitter that was deployed in the sealed bomb bays of the four-engine American Boeing B-17 Flying Fortresses. The Mandrel system was interesting in that it had been designed specifically to jam the German Freya and Wurzburg radar systems and was used by aircraft of the RAF's No.100 Group of Bomber Command. It was formed on 11 November 1943 specifically to deal with the development, training and implementation of Britain's use of electronic counter measures. The newly formed group was based at a number of RAF stations throughout East Anglia.

The Piperjack system was an airborne jamming transmitter used by both the B-24 American Liberator and B-17 Flying Fortress heavy bomber, which were also part of No.100 Group, Bomber Command. The way it worked was that the lead aircraft of an attacking bomber stream would carry the jamming transmitter, which formed a shield for the rest of the aircraft in the stream, in effect making them invisible to German radar units on the ground.

What follows are some of the defensive radar systems employed by Germany to defend herself against Allied bombing raids.

Freya radar system

The Freya radar system had a somewhat unusual connection with Norse mythology, in that it was named after the Norse goddess Freyja, who was associated with beauty, fertility, love, sex and war, and rode on a chariot that was pulled by two cats. The Freya system was a long-range early warning radar system which could locate British bombers as they approached German-occupied air space, and direct Luftwaffe fighter aircraft to their location to attack them.

The Freya system was usually deployed in conjunction with Wurzburg, as the latter, although with a much shorter range, was far more accurate. The Freya was the larger and more cumbersome of the two systems, which meant that the Wurzburg was easier and more economical to mass produce: a big advantage when it came to the number of units that were needed to effectively defend Germany and the countries which she occupied. But together, the two systems were a force to be reckoned with.

Wurzburg radar system

The Wurzburg radar system was the main gun laying radar used by Germany's Wehrmacht, Luftwaffe and Army units throughout the Second World War. The term 'gun laying' in this instance refers to an artillery piece being used against an aerial target. It could be used in one of two ways. Firstly, in a direct fire capacity, whereby the ground units would aim and fire directly at a given identifiable target, or secondly, indirect fire where elements such as azimuth, the horizontal plane, elevation, and the vertical plane are calculated and the sights of the weapon are adjusted accordingly. Indirect fire was used when a target could not be seen, but it was known by the sound of the aircraft's engines that enemy aircraft were in the skies above.

As Britain started to recover in the aftermath of the evacuations at Dunkirk, much of her war production was aimed at the RAF's Bomber Command, not only to ensure the skies over Britain were safe, but so that air raids on targets in German and throughout German-occupied Europe could be conducted. During these raids throughout 1941, it was noted that there was a significant increase in the number of British aircraft being lost. The question for the military authorities was how this was happening. Via the hard work of British military intelligence, it was ascertained that the reason for the dramatic increase in losses of RAF bomber aircraft was down to Germany's use of radar equipment.

The initial development work on radar technology had begun in Britain in the early 1930s, much of which had been carried out by Robert Watson-Watt and his assistant, Arnold Frederic Wilkins. The men had first come together whilst working for the Met Office in the early 1920s, with their main area of interest being radio physics. Their work eventually led to the development of what became known by its nickname of the huff-duff system, which stood for high-frequency direction finding.

When eventually deployed for military purposes in the late 1930s, it was used to locate the position of German radios whilst they were sending messages to another location. It had actually been Watts's assistant, Wilkins, who had come up with the idea of using radio signals to locate aircraft at long distances in 1935. The system was also used to great effect in a defensive capacity during the Battle of Britain.

Reginald Victor Jones, who was only 28 years of age at the outbreak of the Second World War, was a British physicist who became the country's first scientific intelligence officer. Despite his time in the early years of the war being spent investigating and researching a comparison between British and German radar technology, there were those in British society who actually questioned whether Germany even had a radar capability.

Jones's research had been helped by the capture of crashed Luftwaffe aircraft, Enigma decryptions, and the interrogations of German prisoners of war. This led him to discover that Germany was transmitting high-frequency radio signals towards Britain. The unknown element of this discovery was the location from where they were being sent.

Throughout 1941, aircraft of the RAF had carried out a number of aerial reconnaissance missions over northern Europe, including France. On one of these missions by a Spitfire from the RAF's No.1 Photographic Reconnaissance Unit, a site on the French coast near Le Havre was spotted and photographed. The photographs revealed a number of what they believed to be small radar installations, but what the photographs couldn't show, was what they were being used for. At the same time the RAF were experiencing heavy losses amongst bomber groups that were taking part in raids against identified land targets throughout German-occupied Europe. The belief amongst some of Britain's top scientific minds was that these installations were somehow connected to the RAF's aerial losses.

This meant that one of these installations had to be inspected to see what its purpose was. There were two ways of achieving this. The first but less practical way was to have a scientist parachuted into a location where one of these radar systems was located, who could then physically examine it. To do this would take a large number of supporting commandos and a great deal of time spent carrying out an inspection of the equipment. German forces were not just going to stand idly by and let this happen without intervening. There was also a strong possibility that in any subsequent 'contact' between the two sides, the scientist could either be captured or killed, meaning that any information he had obtained would be lost. The other option was to send a team to raid a location where one of these radar systems was in place, capture it and bring it back to England so that it could be examined safely and in much greater detail.

The British had previously located a number of similar sites in France, as well as in other German-occupied territories, but these were further inland which made them more difficult to even consider, whilst the most recent find was literally on a coastal cliff top just outside the French village of Bruneval. Such a location provided the best possibility of the raid being successful. Identifying the site at Bruneval as the most suitable location from where a

Wurzburg radar system could be successfully retrieved, was the easy bit. The hard part was obtaining official permission for the raid to be carried out.

At the time the commander of Combined Operations was Admiral Lord Louis Mountbatten, and it was on his desk that the request for permission for the raid to go ahead fell. He liked the idea in principle, but needed the approval of the Chiefs of Staff Committee. Mountbatten outlined the idea as it had been presented to him, adding his own endorsement to it and the committee, impressed with what they had heard, approved it.

Next was the planning stage. After closely examining the location of the Wurzburg radar installation, it quickly became apparent that any raid from the sea was out of the question, because of the heavy defensive fortifications which surrounded it. The main risk was that the element of surprise would be lost as soon as the raiding party hit the beach, and that the journey from there to the location of the radar installation would be carried out under sustained and heavy enemy fire, which meant that the British casualty count was more than likely going to be high.

It was decided that for the raid to have the greatest chance of success, the best course of action would be to carry out an airborne assault on the installation, therefore providing any attacking force with the element of surprise, more likelihood of the raid being successful, and a reduction in the number of casualties they would sustain.

The raid then didn't just simultaneously happen. The men who were to be sent on the mission first had to be selected, then undergo specific and detailed training to give themselves every opportunity of successfully carrying out the raid and returning home safely. Those chosen to carry out the mission were 120 men of 'C' Company, 2nd Parachute Battalion, of the 1st Airborne Division of the British Army, who were under the direct command of Major John Frost. The unit had only been formed in late 1941 at the insistence of Winston Churchill, and Operation Biting was their first mission. The man in overall charge of this newly formed unit was Major General Frederick A.M. Browning.

The choice of men from 'C' Company to carry out the raid caused some concern, because Major Frost and his men had not actually completed their parachute training course. If you think that was unusual, then give some consideration to the high level of secrecy which had been placed on the planning of the actual raid. Initially not even Major Frost knew that such a raid was going to take place. He had a meeting with a liaison officer from the 1st Airborne Division's headquarters, who informed him that he and his men were to take part in a pre-arranged airborne warfare demonstration for members of the War Cabinet. But when he was told that 'C' Company would be split into four sections for the exercise, he was not entirely happy, as it would not be a tactic he would deploy operationally. Frost took the matter further and raised his objections with a more senior officer, who was also a member of the 1st Airborne Division's headquarters. It was only when he was informed the exercise was actually part of the training for the proposed raid on Saint-Jouin-Bruneval, a coastal village in the Normandy region of France, known by the codename Operation Biting, that he withdrew his objection. He did not, however, inform his men of the real intention of the exercise.

'C' Company's training was split between Salisbury Plain in Wiltshire and Loch Fyne at Inveraray in Scotland, where they practised all aspects of the impending operation. These included night-time embarkations on landing craft, which was to replicate the immediate aftermath of the operation where they would be evacuated from the beach, hopefully with one of the Wurzburg radar units in their possession. After completing their training in Scotland they returned to Wiltshire, where they underwent parachute training with the actual aircraft and aircrew they would be using on the raid.

The final part of the training saw Major Frost and his men looking over a scale model of the radar installation at Bruneval and the surrounding buildings. This helped them all build a mental picture of what they would come across on the actual raid. During this time Major Frost was introduced to a number of significant people who would be connected to the raid. One of them was Flight Sergeant C.W.H. Cox, who had volunteered to be the man who would accompany 'C' Company on the raid, inspect the Wurzburg radar, photograph it, and dismantle part of it so that it could be removed and taken back to the UK. Much to everybody's surprise, the War Office refused permission for Cox to be allowed to wear Army uniform on the raid, which meant that if captured, it would not have taken the Germans long to work out the important part he had played.

The raid itself was a combined effort and required teamwork of the highest order to be a success. Besides Major Frost and his men who were the brave and daring souls who carried out the actual raid, along with Flight Sergeant Cox, there were other units of men without whose efforts the raid could not have gone ahead. They included the RAF's aircraft and crews of No.51 Squadron, led by Wing Commander Percy Charles Pickard, who had the task of dropping off the raiding party at the correct location close to the installation at Bruneval. There were also elements of the Royal Australian Navy, led by Commander F.N. Cook, who were responsible for evacuating the raiding party after they had completed their mission. Also on the mission were thirty-two officers and men of No.12 Commando, who would be on the landing craft on which Major Frost and his men would be evacuated. Their purpose was to provide covering fire against any Germans who had managed to follow the raiding party down to the beach. A ten-man section, led by Lieutenant Dennis Vernon, from 1st Air Troop, Royal Engineers, were to dismantle the Wurzburg radar and lay a number of mines to prevent the Germans from bringing up vehicular support such as tanks.

Extremely important for the success of the raid was the help provided by the French Resistance, in particular Gilbert Renault, who had provided detailed information to the British about German deployments at the Bruneval radar installation. This knowledge was invaluable and without it the raid could not have gone ahead. It may well have been the RAF who had provided photographs of the installation which provided a visual layout of it and its buildings, but it was Renault and his colleagues who provided the finite detail of the number of German soldiers and technicians who were deployed there.

From the German perspective, it must have been somewhat of a strange scenario. It was obviously a location they had to try their best to protect, but the last thing they would expect was a physical assault on their position by ground troops.

A radar installation such as the one at Bruneval would require technicians provided by the Luftwaffe on site twenty-four hours a day, as well as soldiers from the German Army to protect them. The way that the defensive pillboxes and machine-gun positions were set up along the cliff top suggests that if they were expecting an infantry attack, then it was from the beach and not inland. The beach immediately below the radar instillation was not mined, although regular foot patrols were maintained.

After the raid had been postponed on a couple of occasions due to adverse weather conditions, it finally went ahead on the evening of 27 February 1942. An Armstrong Whitworth A W 38 Whitley, a twin-engined aircraft which was usually deployed as a medium bomber, took off from RAF Thruxton, near Andover in Hampshire, carrying Major Frost and his men from 'C' Company. As the aircraft approached the French coast, it encountered heavy Flak from German defensive coastal positions, but no major damage was sustained.

With the drop having been made and the Whitley on its way back to the UK, Major Frost gathered his men, checked that they had all their equipment, before making the short journey on foot to their intended target. The villa that housed the radar was taken without too much trouble after a brief exchange of gunfire.

In what would be classed as a commando style raid, there were three important parts to the operation for it to have any chance of being successful. Firstly, was the planning stage, which had to result in every man knowing what part he had to play. This was only possible with repetitive training so that what the men were training for almost became second nature to them. Once this had been achieved and the operation had begun, the two remaining elements that were needed were speed and surprise.

Two Germans were captured at the villa and taken prisoner, but the raiding party was then attacked by soldiers from the adjoining buildings as they began their escape towards the beach. During this exchange one of the British soldiers was shot and killed. As the raiding party reached the beach, it was clear that the men who had been allocated the job of securing that area had been unsuccessful, as one of the German machine guns opened up, wounding one of the British soldiers.

Eventually the enemy threat on the beach was neutralised. The members of the raiding party, along with the sappers who had landed with them, had acquired the radar equipment they had come for and waited on the beach to be evacuated. Like all such operations, not everything always goes according to plan and Operation Biting was no different. During the operation there were radio problems which prevented any of the different sections involved in the raid from being able to communicate with each other, and when it came time for them to head to the beach in the early hours of 28 February to be evacuated, Major Frost was unable to make radio contact with the naval vessels that were waiting to pick up him and his men and take them back across the English Channel. This left the British forces in a perilous position, as it would not be long before German reinforcements arrived at the Bruneval radar installation and if Frost and his men were still on the beach, they would probably have been killed or captured and the mission would have failed. However Major Frost had one of his men fire off an emergency signal flare which did its job, as not long after six Allied landing craft arrived to evacuate those who had taken part in the operation, along with the much-prized Wurzburg radar unit. The arrival of the landing craft was timely as large numbers of German soldiers had begun amassing on the cliff top above their position.

Such was the importance of the captured Wurzburg radar that allowing the Germans to retrieve it was not an option, no matter what the cost in human life. Of Major Frost's men, two were killed, another eight were wounded and a further six were captured by the Germans. To ensure that the parts of the Wurzburg radar and those involved in the operation arrived safely back at Portsmouth, they had an escort of four destroyers and a number of Spitfires.

The Commonwealth War Graves Commission records that two British soldiers who were killed in action on 28 February 1942 were buried at the Ste. Marie Cemetery at Le

Havre, approximately 12 miles from Saint-Jouin-Bruneval. The two men in question were Private 5347681 Alan Worton Scott (24) a member of the 9th Battalion, Royal Berkshire Regiment, and Rifleman 3252284 Hugh Duncan McDonald McIntyre (28) a member of the 9th Battalion, Cameronians (Scottish Rifles). At the time of their deaths, both men were attached to the 2nd Battalion, The Parachute Regiment, Army Air Corps.

If proof were needed to determine whether the raid had been a success or not, it came the following day when an RAF Hurricane made its way across the English Channel and flew over the radar installation at Bruneval undetected, before the Germans realised what was happening, showing quite clearly the importance of radar as an early warning system.

The technical knowledge gleaned by the capture of the Wurzburg radar by British scientists was of immense importance. Its design was simple in that it was modular, built by a number of parts that were not only easy to replace, but which could be used in different radar systems. This meant that if any of the parts required replacing, not only was it a relatively straight forward procedure, but much easier to do than it would be on a comparative British radar unit.

British scientists also discovered that to 'blind' a Wurzburg radar system in any future bombing operations in countries throughout German-occupied Europe, the aircraft would have to deploy a recently developed British counter measure, known as 'Window', which came in the form of thin pieces of aluminium, and would confuse radar operators as to what they were actually seeing on their screens.

There were two other unexpected pluses that came out of the capture of the Wurzburg radar system. Britain's own radar research and development up until this point of the Second World War, was carried out by the Telecommunications Research Establishment, located at the coastal town of Swanage in Dorset. To ensure it wasn't as vulnerable to attack as the installation at Bruneval had been, it was moved 170 miles inland to Malvern in Worcestershire.

In the aftermath of the British raid, the Germans reviewed the defences of their radar installation at Bruneval. Surprisingly, they decided to keep it in place. But for Britain and her Allies, what was possibly even better was the decision by the Germans to place rings of barbed wire around all the radar units at each radar installation. Despite any defensive benefit which this action might well have provided, it was also of great benefit to the Allies, whose aircraft were easily able to spot them, making them much easier targets. This was particularly helpful in the lead up to the Allied invasion of German-occupied Europe in June 1944.

The following is an article that appeared in the *Nottingham Journal* dated 18 May 1942, concerning photographs of the area of Bruneval.

Photographs taken during a holiday contributed largely to the success of the Bruneval raid, a member of the naval staff disclosed in a broadcast yesterday.

When every possible source of information about the Bruneval area had been thoroughly combed for details, we still needed an actual picture of the few hundred yards of France where the German radiolocation centre was situated to complete the information needed.

Quite by chance it was found that one of the staff officers working on the plan had spent a holiday in the Bruneval neighbourhood just before the war. In an album stored away in a trunk at his home he found photographs taken on his holiday showing in minute detail the exact spot involved.

It was five of these photographs put together which forged the last link in the plan.

Was this an early example of intentional misinformation? It was noticeable that in the above article, written just two months after the raid, there is neither a name afforded to the mysterious staff officer who had supposedly taken holiday snaps of the Bruneval area, nor any mention of the RAF pilots who had flown over the area and taken a number of detailed photographs of it in the weeks leading up to the actual raid.

An interesting article appeared in the *Western Mail* dated 24 February 1947.

Professor's story of Bruneval Raid

Some of the top secret stories of how British scientists, working in collaboration with secret agents, and assisted by daring RAF photographic pilots, helped to smash the German night defence system in the last war, were told last week by Professor R.V. Jones of the Chair of Natural Philosophy at Aberdeen University, in a lecture to Service chiefs and Whitehall heads.

In his lecture Professor Jones gave an account of his war work as Director of Scientific Intelligence at the Air Ministry. His work won the appreciation of Mr Churchill and Lord Cherwell, the famous scientist. Professor Jones described the famous Bruneval raid as one of the thrusts in the intelligence attack on the German night defences.

The raid depended on a photograph, and this is the dramatic story behind it as told by the professor. After a chase extended from the Black Sea to the English Channel one of Professor Jones's staff found a small speck on a photograph, so small that they had to examine several photographs to prove that it was not a speck of dust.

The next stage was to get the speck photographed. This was done by Squadron Leader Tony Hill. Hill's photographs were among the classics of the war and led directly to the Bruneval raid. He subsequently took nearly all the most dangerous low oblique photographs of the radar stations wanted by the intelligence.

It was interesting that Professor Jones was allowed to give such a lecture, including what he did during the war, just two years after it had finished. One would have assumed that such information was still not for public consumption under the Official Secrets Act.

Squadron leader Tony Hill was killed in action whilst photographing the area of Le Creusot in southeast France, on 18 October 1942. When his aircraft hit the ground the impact broke his back. Members of the French Resistance managed to get to his downed aircraft before the Germans did, and hid him. On 12 November 1942, an RAF aircraft which had flown from England, landed at a small airstrip in France to pick him up and take him back to England. He died as he was being carried to the aircraft.

The following is what Professor Jones had to say about Hill's death:

> *Squadron-leader Hill died in a German hospital of wounds received while photographing Le Creusot in 1942. We owe him a very great debt for his skill, courage, and enterprise. He was the greatest low oblique photographer of the war,' said Professor Jones.*

> *Continuing his story of the Bruneval raid, Professor Jones said that its success finally depended on an RAF radio mechanic Flight Sergeant C.W.H. Fox who parachuted at Bruneval. It was only Flight Sergeant Cox's coolness and skill in dismantling the Wurzburg apparatus, which he had never seen, in the dark and under fire, that made the Bruneval raid the outstanding success it was.*

A recent film, "School for Secrets" at least implied that it was due to a civilian scientist. While a civilian scientist did go on the seaborne part of the raid, none would like to steal the credit from Flight Sergeant's splendid performance.

The *Aberdeen Press and Journal* newspaper, also dated 24 February 1947, covered the same story about Professor Jones's lecture, which also included the following anecdote:

Continuing his story of the Bruneval raid, Professor Jones says that its success finally depended on an RAF radio mechanic, Flight Sergeant C.W.H. Cox, who had never previously been out of England, on the sea, or in the air, but who volunteered for a dangerous operation, and after a short training, parachuted at Bruneval.

In the final briefing Professor Jones warned Flight Sergeant Cox of the danger of being specially interrogated if taken prisoner, and, above all, to be careful of any German officer who was unexpectedly kind to him.

Flight Sergeant Cox stood to attention, and said; "I can stand a lot of kindness sir."

It was only Flight Sergeant Cox's coolness and skill in dismantling the Wurzburg apparatus, which he had never seen in the dark and under fire, that made the Bruneval raid the outstanding success it was.

Professor Jones told many stories during his lecture in London, one in particular was particularly relevant as it concerned an agent whom he had asked to locate German searchlight units in Belgium.

> *Instead of laboriously going round the countryside finding them, he broke into the hut of the German officer commanding searchlights over literally half of Belgium, and secured his map showing the positions of every searchlight and radar station under his command. That was an enormous help. It, in fact, provided one of the most vital clues in the entire intelligence picture.*
>
> *This information culminated at the end of 1942 in a complete knowledge of the German defence system as it was. From then on they could say exactly what counter measures they were always able to follow, and at times anticipate it. Once they had found the scientific principles and technical details employed in the equipment of the German night defences, all the other intelligence, such as order of battle, deployment, and so forth, fell into place.*

What a fillip that was for the British and American bomber making their way to German-occupied Europe on a raid, and how frustrating must that have been for the Germans.

CHAPTER 10

Newspaper Articles

It was clear that Germany had been planning for the Second World many years before it began. After Adolf Hitler became Chancellor of Germany on 30 January 1933, the Nazi Party quickly came to dominance.

The *Liverpool Echo* included an interesting article in its edition of 19 October 1933.

German Air Defences – A Decree Issued Today
Income Tax Relief – If Bombproof Cellars are Provided

The serial defence of Germany in case of emergency is the object of a decree published by Count Schwerin von Krosigh, the minister of Finance. All money expended by private individuals or firms for advancing Germany's protection from air attacks can be deducted in total from the income when making income or Corporation tax returns. The decree says:

"By the Treaty of Versailles, Germany was forbidden military planes. We are denied, therefore

the most effective weapon against air attacks. All the greater importance, therefore, attaches to the civil air protection measures calculated to safeguard the population against danger from the air.

In the interests of the population as well as of national defence, such measures must therefore be most widely encouraged by a policy of tax deduction. The air protection primarily concerns industrial undertakings, businesses with large numbers of employees, and house owners.

The building of gas and bomb proof cellars, the purchase of gas masks, the installation of alarm arrangements, and the drilling of special squads in the use of defensive instruments are suggested by the ministry."

It is unclear why, or who posed such a military threat to Germany in 1933 that she would have to consider building air raid shelters. Six years before the war, here were the German authorities preparing for war. The only fighting that they were involved in was internally, as the Nazi party rose to power and fought to rid the country of political opponents. They had no external enemies, so the only sensible conclusion that can be drawn is that this was the beginning of their own journey to war, a war they had planned for and a war that they wanted. The order about the bombproof cellars was an insurance policy for the future, should things not go according to plan.

The *Sunderland Daily Echo and Shipping Gazette* dated 17 April 1934, printed an article which included the same question I have asked amidst the pages of this chapter.

German Air Defences

The German Note explaining the reasons for the increased estimates for national defence in reality adds very little to the facts which were known in this country. There is greater detail and the statement of the German Foreign Minister indicated that the 50% increase in naval estimates is due to the need for renovation of obsolete units. The military changes, namely, the conversion of the long service Army into a more numerous force of short service men, was a provision urged upon Germany by the Disarmament Conference, therefore no criticism can be directed to this change.

However, the trebling of the estimates for air services and defences, indicates a surprising determination to make wholesale defences against air invasion. It is necessary to ask against whom such provisions are being made? Air transport is being modernised, splinter and gas proof cellars are being provided and units are being trained in poison gas defensive measure. Such steps are typical of traditional German thoroughness and organization.

Yet is it right that a nation should squander huge sums in preparation for imaginary dangers, while unable to meet its foreign debts, and facing domestic problems, one of which is acute unemployment?

The question quite naturally may be asked, what limit, if any, is Germany setting herself in defensive measures. The huge increases in this year's estimates may be but a beginning.

Germany has called for equality of armaments, and failing concession of the demand, this may be her way of making sure that she does not lack preparation for defence if not offence.

Certain it is that no neighbouring nation desires to attack her for mere territorial gain. Then why this aerial defensive preparation far in advance, we believe, by any other European country.

It is quite startling to think that Nazi Germany was looking at such aspects in so much detail, yet it does not seem to have raised much in the way of concern amongst the British, French or American authorities, especially as there was no known threat to her state as a sovereign nation.

The *Aberdeen Press and Journal* newspaper of 12 January 1938 included a very interesting report about a visit to Berlin by a Mr Geoffrey Lloyd.

Mr Geoffrey Lloyd to Study German Air Defences

The Home Office announces that in accordance with arrangements made shortly before Christmas,

Mr Geoffrey Lloyd, Parliamentary Under Secretary, Home Office, will visit Berlin on January 18 for the purpose of studying certain points in the German air raid precautions organisation which have emerged from previous visits, for which facilities were given to officials of the Air Raids Precautions Department by the German Government. On his return journey Mr Lloyd will pay a visit to Paris for a similar purpose.

Why would a serving Conservative Member of Parliament, and the British Under Secretary of State for the Home Department, pay a visit to the German capital to check that all was well with their air raid precautions? Why would Germany allow such a visit to take place, when by then it must have been obvious to both sides that in any future war, it was more than likely that they would be on opposite sides. One would have thought that he would have been best served by checking on Britain's air raid precautions, rather than those of an expectant enemy.

On 11 July 1939 twelve squadrons of aircraft from the RAF took part in a training exercise over France. More than 100 bombers and some 400 men were involved in the cross-channel exercise, which covered a total of 120,000 miles flown at cruising speed. Eight squadrons of medium bombers each flew a distance of 800 miles between Cherbourg, Le Tréport, Orléans and Le Mans in just under four hours. A further two squadrons of heavy bombers, took off from their base in the Midlands, flew across the English Channel to an un-named destination in southwestern France. This saw the British aircraft fly a distance between 1,000 and 1,200 miles in a time of around six and a half hours. Later the same day, two more heavy bomber squadrons flew the same route, taking them approximately seven hours.

The purpose of the flights was to give the crews involved, the experience of navigation on long flights in the skies over Europe. In response to these flights the German Air Ministry made the following announcement.

> *"Germany may rest calmly assured that not one of the British bombers would get through the German air defences," the Lokal Anzeiger says, referring to the comment attributed to a Paris newspaper that the long-distance flight of British bombers over France would give the population of Nuremberg, Leipzig and Hamburg food for thought. The "Lokal Anzeiger"* [a Berlin based newspaper] *describes this comment as a provocation, and heads its comment, "playing with fire."*

On 11 October 1939, an article appeared in the *Birmingham Daily Post* under the heading of 'The War in the Air'. It was a long article which covered different aspects of the war, one of which is relevant to this book:

> *Bomber Command has carried out the great series of "leaflet raids" into Germany and reconnaissance flights over and beyond the Siegfried Line which*

have provoked no effectual opposition from the German air defences. Things cannot remain so easy for the RAF.

An interesting article appeared in the *Dundee Evening Telegraph*, of 13 September 1940.

German 'Flak' has Little Success Against RAF

Almost every pilot who returns from a raid over Germany or enemy occupied territory makes some reference to "Flak" in his report. He may record that "Flak" was either heavy or light, accurate or inaccurate, intense or moderate, or, if his luck is in, then there was no "Flak".

"Flak" is in fact what used to be called in the last war "Archie", "Ack-Ack" or anti-aircraft fire. The name comes from the German initials F.L.A.K, "Flieger Abwehr Kanone", or the gun that drives off raiders.

In these days of high flying and mass raids, anti-aircraft gunnery is a more complicated and varied business than it was in the last war, and the Flak intelligence experts at the War Ministry have recently issued for the information of those concerned a "Strangers' Guide to Flak". This guide shows, in convenient and readily grasped form, the range, calibre, weight type of shell, and rate of fire.

"There are two principal kinds of Flak, light and heavy. Light Flak are guns of calibres between three-quarters of an inch and two inches. The weight of the shell increases from less than half a lb. in the case of the smallest of the guns to three and one-third lb. in the case of the 47 mm.

The rate of fire decreases as the range, weight of shell and calibre increase. The German 20 mm, for example, fires about 160 rounds a minute up to 7,000 feet, while the 47 mm, fires 25 rounds a minute to a height of more than three miles.

Light Flak fire tracer shells, which burst on impact, have self-destroying detonators. That is to say that they explode in the air, even if they miss their target and, therefore, cannot fall back and explode on the ground.

Heavy Flak do not fire tracers. They fire time fused shells, and range from the 15 rounds a minute, 75 mm guns throwing shells to 20,000 feet to the 105 mm guns firing ten 32-pounder shells a minute to 30,000."

Why the Air Ministry deemed it necessary to produce a 'Strangers' Guide to Flak' for public consumption is unknown, and why they believed the public would want to have such detailed information about this weapon is even more difficult to fathom. The War Ministry did not provide such information for a Lee Enfield .303 rifle, a Churchill tank, or a Spitfire aircraft, so why the inclination to provide it for anti-aircraft weaponry? It is doubtful that anyone with a relative serving with the RAF, or the Royal Air Force Volunteer Reserve, would want to read such detailed information about the weapons that were being fired by German air defences at the aircraft their loved ones were flying in.

Fire Control

The method of fire control differs between light and heavy Flak. Light Flak is directed by a speed and course sight. Heavy Flak is controlled by a predictor, the complicated instrument with which eleven men obtain for the gunner all the data necessary in theory for the shell to meet its target, if, in the interval between the firing of the gun and the arrival of the shell at the point of prediction the aircraft has not changed direction, height or speed. Normally an aircraft encountering Flak would continue to change at least one of these factors.

At night or in cloud, Flak fire can be directed by sound locators, but this method is naturally much less accurate than visual shooting.

Our own anti-aircraft batteries possess guns equivalent to, or better than the German Flak. It is encouraging to note that while our "Ack-Ack" batteries have scored many successes over Germany's fighters and bombers in recent raids, our own aircraft frequently fly home after having passed through intense heavy or light Flak barrages. Occasionally shells have actually passed through their wings or fuselages.

The *Derby Daily Telegraph*, dated 21 September 1940, included the following article taken from an announcement made by Bremen radio. This was a well-documented incident with similar articles also appearing the same day in many other newspapers:

Bremen Radio admitted this morning that RAF planes entered Central Germany last night. The station's announcer said: "Last night two waves of British planes attempted to attack Hamburg and Berlin. Thanks to the German air defences they were turned back. A group of enemy planes which attempted to enter Germany from the Heligoland Bight, were forced to turn back over the Elbe Estuary by Germany anti-aircraft fire and fighter aircraft.

A further group of British planes succeeded in entering Central Germany. They were engaged by a strong German air barrage in the province of Hanover. When German fighters took off from their bases, the British planes turned tail.

During night attacks by single British aircraft on towns in Western Germany, several houses were destroyed and a church and a cemetery were hit. Thirteen civilians were killed and a great number injured.

From a propaganda perspective, Germany and Britain were always going to have a different version of the same events. That was part and parcel of war. Neither side, although willing to admit that attacks had taken place, wanted to report too much about such events, because of the fear of affecting public morale. Both sides only wanted to highlight positive news stories, because an important element of the war was keeping the general public 'on side' and that was never going to be achieved if they repeatedly reported the true facts of such events, especially if they were not good. Churchill had witnessed this at first hand, after Neville Chamberlain was forced to resign as the British Prime minister in May 1940, after he had 'dithered' in giving Germany an ultimatum over their invasion of Poland and had overseen a British military disaster in Norway.

The *Sunday Post* of 16 November 1941, included the following interesting article in relation to the effectiveness of German anti-aircraft batteries.

Not one British Raid on European Coast – Says Berlin

The Germans last night issued a semi-official statement congratulating themselves that Britain has not "succeeded in carrying out one large scale operation" on the Continent. This is due it says, to the extremely effective German air defences.

From the Spanish coast, along the French, Belgian and Dutch coasts, northwards past Denmark and its

islands, and along the whole Norwegian coast, vast
numbers of artillery pieces and flak batteries are
stationed today. Naval and air bases here complete
the defences of this 6,000-kilometre coastline.

Making such a claim could have quite easily come across as
a red rag to a bull, a gauntlet thrown down in the face of the
British establishment both in a political and military sense.
However, the claim was not correct as the RAF had carried
out a bombing raid on Berlin on 25 August 1940, and there
had also been a French raid there on 7 June 1940.

A solitary French bomber aircraft piloted by navy
Captain Henri Daillière, and named the *Jules Verne* after
the famous French explorer, flew to Berlin to carry out
an attack on the Siemens factory in the Tegel area of the
city. They flew in low to drop their bombs and luckily were
not caught in the after blast of the detonations. Two of the
plane's crew took to dropping their small incendiary bombs
by hand as the aircraft wasn't equipped to jettison them
mechanically. They had somehow managed to miss the
attention of German defensive batteries, especially those
situated around the city's Tempelhof airport.

It was only when their bombs exploded that the *Jules
Verne* and her crew came to the attention of the German
air defences, which suddenly sparked into life. No sooner
had the sirens sounded, indicating that an enemy raid was
underway, than the beams of the powerful searchlights
lit up the night sky as they searched for a target. This in
turn saw the anti-aircraft guns spew out their molten lead

bullets in an uncoordinated response. They could not see their intended target, but instead fired blindly towards the sound of the *Jules Verne* aircraft, her crew by now no doubt praying that they would be able to escape before they were struck by exploding shrapnel.

News of this raid on the nation's capital was supressed from the German public by the country's propaganda ministry, which claimed that the incident had been nothing more than an air raid drill, in preparation for such an enemy attack.

A humorous anecdote about this raid on Berlin involved the German Air Minister, Hermann Göring, who before the war, in one of his buffoon-like moments, had stated that, 'If any bombs fall on the Reich, I will change my name to Maier.' This was a reference to the fact that it was a common German name, such as 'Smith' would be in English. There is no such record indicating that Göring ever held true to his word.

The attack on Berlin on 25 August 1940 by some seventy British bombers, was an act of retaliation ordered by Winston Churchill and his War Cabinet in response to a German aircraft having dropped bombs on London whilst on its way home from a bombing raid, which had seen a number of bombs dropped at Manston and Ramsgate in Kent resulting in the deaths of twenty-nine British civilians. At the time Hitler had issued an order to the Luftwaffe that London was not to be attacked, possibly in the hope that Britain would reciprocate by not conducting similar raids on Berlin.

The *Fife Free Press & Kirkcaldy Guardian* newspaper dated 13 December 1941, included this article:

In the Air

We are right in continuing our policy of planned in advance strategic bombing of German centres of production, and that our almost daily sweeps over occupied territories are well worthwhile.

We have to face the fact however, that German air defences have also improved, and, whilst we would be the last to suggest that heavy losses such as we have experienced on several occasions of late should by themselves be regarded as a reason for changed tactics, the fact does remain that unless one can be convinced that these tactics are right, it is questionable whether we should continue to run the risks which we do.

The *Yorkshire Post and Leeds Intelligence* newspaper of 13 February 1942 included an article about the bombing of Japan and how it might be carried out. By way of a comparison of the risks involved, mention was made of the Allied bombing of Germany.

Japan, then is within reach of the latest large bombers from bases which are available to the united nations. The point is, what bomb load could be carried and what would be the risks of such a flight?

The bomb load would be smaller than is carried, for instance, by the RAF to Brest. But it would still be a useful load. It would be a bigger load than was carried by the Wellingtons and Whitleys during our own early bombing of Germany. So it comes down to the risks involved for the damage done. In my opinion the risks of such a long flight are lower than the present risks of piercing German air defences over Germany. German air defences have been greatly improved and our bomber captains and crews say that the flak is intense and accurate. To get to their objectives entails going through heavy fire and often facing enemy night fighters.

They may have only two or three hundred miles out and back, a total of four or six hundred miles to go over enemy territory, and that is a short distance compared with the distance that would have to be flown if the attempt were made to bomb Japan.

One of the strangest articles concerning German air defences was recorded on the back page of the *Staffordshire Sentinel* on 26 June 1943. The article was unusual was because it appeared on the newspaper's sports page and was only one of two about non-sporting matters.

German Air Defences

More than 1,000 fighter planes and 30,000 AA guns are concentrated to protect North-West Germany, said Mr Elmer Davis, Director of Office of War Information, in Washington today.

The *Birmingham Mail* dated 1 September 1943 carried an in-depth report concerning an RAF attack on Berlin the previous night.

Berlin Again – Another Pounding by RAF. Great weight of Bombs Dropped – Large Fires

Berlin received another big pounding last night, when large formations of our heavy bombers were over the city. The following communique was issued by the Air Ministry today:

Last night a great weight of high explosive and incendiary bombs was dropped on Berlin in 45 minutes. Broken cloud at low levels made it difficult to assess results visually, but large fires were seen, and the indications are that great damage was done. The enemy put up very large fighter forces over the capital and its approaches, in an unsuccessful attempt to prevent the launching of a concentrated attack. A number of his aircraft were destroyed in combat.

Airfields and other targets in France and the Low Countries were also attacked during the night. Forty-seven bombers and one fighter are missing.

By the time it was all over a total of 47 British aircraft were not accounted for along with a single fighter, meaning that somewhere in the region of 330 British airmen were either lost or captured. The Commonwealth War Graves Commission records that 330 men of the RAF lost their lives on the night of 31 August to 1 September 1943.

An un-named captain of one of the British bombers which took part in the raid, said:

Flak was moderate, but many enemy fighters

It was a tense and exciting struggle from the moment we crossed the enemy coast. Enemy fighters were on patrol along the whole route and my gunners could not relax for an instant until we were over the sea again. We were one of the first to arrive, and as we approached the capital, the defences were just coming into action. Hundreds of searchlights were turned on, but they were not so effective as usual because of scattered cloud over the city. We found a gap and dropped our bombs and we turned away. It was about five minutes after the attack had started, there was a very big explosion that went off with an orange flash.

A crew member of one of the British bombers on the night in question was Pilot officer 144714 George Albert Scarcliffe, who was acting as a rear gunner. This was his account of the raid:

"I have not been to Berlin since last year," he said, "and since then there has been a great change in the defences. Last year I took part in two attacks on the capital and in those days there seemed even more guns

there than in the Ruhr, but very few fighters. Now it
is the other way round. There were bags of fighters
last night but the flak was really only moderate.

We were attacked three times by fighters. The first
was a Junkers 88, and shortly after we had driven it
off we were attacked by two single engine aircraft.
My captain out-manoeuvred them and we went on
and bombed."

George Albert Scarcliffe, who was a member of the Royal
Air Force Volunteer Reserve, serving with No.78 Squadron,
was killed in action just six days later on 7 September 1943,
whilst on a bombing raid over Germany. At the time of
his death, he was just 20 years of age and was buried at
Durnbach War Cemetery, in Southern Germany.

The pilot of another aircraft involved in the same
operation, described his memory of the raid as follows:

There was a lot of cloud along the route, but it began
to thin out as we approached Berlin. Presently, far
ahead of us, we could see a faint glow that grew
stronger and stronger as we went on. Through the
gaps in the clouds over the capital we could see the
fires. My bomb aimer called out over the inter-
communication that he dropped the load in the
middle of one of them, and then we turned for home.
The glow of the fires was still visible when we were
70 miles on our homeward journey.

The official German News Agency's version of the raid, which they referred to as a 'terror raid', was, as might be expected, somewhat different.

Last night a new British terror raid was made on Berlin. Newly re-organised German air defences inflicted extremely heavy losses on the raiders. The British bomber formations were dispersed and were forced to jettison most of their bombs. Thanks to the efficient defence, the concentrated attack by the British bombers was frustrated. Above and below the clouds heavy air combats developed, in the course of which numerous British bombers were shot down. The total British losses cannot yet be estimated. It is already certain however, that the German air defences, flak and night fighters alike, have inflicted very heavy losses on the RAF.

The German News Agency would later claim that the number of British bombers shot down by their air defences was 30. This announcement was followed soon after by a German High Command communiqué:

Last night strong British air formations again attacked the area of Greater Berlin. Our night bombers, in co-operation with anti-aircraft and searchlight batteries, disturbed the enemy bomber formations and the intended concentration effect of the raid was thwarted. In some districts of the city and in the vicinity of the capital damage was caused, some of it considerable. The population suffered slight casualties. Enemy nuisance raiders flying singly also dropped bombs at random on some places in Germany.

The last couple of paragraphs of that announcement were vague and told only a part of the story, one that was favourable to assist with keeping the morale of the German people as high as possible. The agency would later report:

Air defence forces brought down 47 British bombers, according to reports so far to hand. Eight more planes were lost by the enemy over the occupied territories in the west yesterday.

The *Liverpool Daily Post* of 22 September 1943, included this article:

Saturated Nazi Defences – Methodical Destruction

The American system of daylight bombing gives great accuracy on specific targets, and is also accompanied by very severe fighting, producing heavy losses among the enemy. The British and American forces are fed by an ever broadening and improving supply of new aircraft, which altogether exceeds the corresponding German aircraft supply by more than four to one.

The continued progress of Anglo-American preponderance, which can certainly be expected month after month, opens the possibility of saturating the German defences, both on the ground and in the air. This word "saturation" has a particular significance in the general field of the air war. If a certain degree of saturation can be reached, and we can be sure that this can only be won against an increasingly hard foe after a bitter struggle with the enemy air defences, a reaction of the most far-reaching character will be produced.

We shall, in fact, create conditions in which, with small loss to ourselves, the actual methodical destruction by day and night of every military target of significance in the widest sense will become possible.

An interesting, but brief, article appeared in the *Gloucestershire Echo* of 11 December 1943. It was a good example of how an event could be reported in two totally different ways.

Mosquitos Attack Germany

An Air Ministry communiqué states that last night Mosquitos of Bomber Command without loss, attacked objectives in Western Germany. The German News Agency today reported: "Enemy planes were over Western Germany during last night.

During sorties of a few enemy planes in daylight on
December 10 over the Dutch-German frontier area
and during nuisance attacks on Western Germany
last night, the German air defences brought down
six enemy aircraft."

The Commonwealth War Graves Commission records that
on 10 December 1943, 18 members of the Royal Air Force
or the Royal Air Force Volunteer Reserve were killed or had
died of their wounds. Of these only four men were buried
in Holland or Germany. On 11 December 1943, the figures
were 27, but none of these were buried in either Holland
or Germany. These figures would suggest that the German
News Agency had been somewhat economical with the
truth.

The *Newcastle Evening Chronicle* newspaper dated
14 January 1944, included the following article:

Germans' 'Balloon' Bombs

Trailing balloon bombs were used for the first time by
German air defences against American bombers in
Tuesday's great air battle over Germany, according
to German overseas radio states Reuter. The new
weapon is to be "reserved for the most important
operations," said a Berlin military spokesman,
quoted by the Berlin correspondent of a Swedish
newspaper. The Germans use a "new type" of quick-
climbing fighter to tow the bombs.

How it Works

German radio gave this account of Tuesday's engagement: "These trailing bombs, or air mines as the German experts call them, were towed by fighters through the attacking bomber squadrons at a height of about 13,000 feet and at a speed of about 130 mph. The method employed was rather similar to that used when towing gliders. These air mines were then released from the tow ropes at the most suitable moment, with a most devastating effect."

The US flying forts were either caught in the two ropes or got with range of the terrific blast from the exploding mines. The German fighters then found easy prey among the bombers.

Germans' Strategic Air Reserve

"Special German air squadrons of a new type will be rushed to defend vital military areas when they are threatened by Allied air fleets in future," says the Berlin correspondent of the German controlled Scandinavian telegraph bureau, quoted by British United Press.

"The Germans have been holding back a considerable strategic air reserve for the big air battles of the war which are now developing," said a German military spokesman according to the correspondent. Our special squadrons will be used for the really vital tasks. They have already proved their value."

The *Manchester Evening News* of 15 January 1944 had a detailed report on an Allied air raid on the German town of Brunswick.

2,000 Tons Dropped in Brunswick Attack
RAF Leave Vital Nazi Air Factories Blazing

Two thousand tons of bombs were dropped last night on Brunswick, important centre of the German aircraft and engineering industry, which was the main target, it was officially announced today, for last night's raids on Germany by Bomber Command. Magdeburg and Berlin were also attacked.

Today's Air Ministry communiqué said large fires were left burning at Brunswick, where the attack was a very heavy one. The communique added Mosquitoes attacked Magdeburg and Berlin, and other aircraft bombed targets in Northern France and laid mines in enemy waters. Thirty-eight of our aircraft are missing.

Brunswick, which is 110 miles west of Berlin, has a population of about 200,000. Of the aircraft factories in and around the town the most important is MIAG (Muhlenau und Industrie AG), making and assembling aircraft components.

Defences Confused

Great confusion must have been produced by Bomber Command's operations among the German air defences, judging by the comments on the attacks put out at first by authorised German sources. One vaguely announced that some of the RAF bombers penetrated as far as Berlin. Another said British bombers flew over Reich territory and met strong German air defences. These comments suggested that our bombers had again fooled the Luftwaffe defenders.

Brunswick was one of the three important targets hit by USAAF heavy bombers in the great daylight attacks on Tuesday. Over 700 Flying Fortresses and Liberators, escorted by Thunderbolts, Lightnings and long-range fighters, then attacked three vital fighter aircraft plants at Brunswick, Oschersleben and Halbertstadt. One of the greatest air battles of the war developed. At Brunswick in that attack, two of the three main assembly buildings producing ME 110s were destroyed, and the third badly hit.

Brunswick also had a number of engineering and armaments works that made artillery tractors, motorcycles and railway signals. The final part of the article shows just what a difficult task Germany had at trying to adequately defend her towns and cities against almost incessant Allied aerial bombardment. No matter what combination of defensive tactics she employed, it was always going to be difficult to sustain a solid defensive capability. Because of the growing number of aircraft the Allies used in their bombing raids, it didn't matter whether she used anti-aircraft guns, barrage balloons, balloon bombs, or fighter aircraft, it was never quite enough to have a sufficient impact on preventing or reducing the number of Allied air raids.

An interesting article about the state of German air defences appeared in the *Newcastle Evening Chronicle* on 10 February 1944:

German Air Defences Inadequate

The once mighty air power of Germany which pounded defenceless Warsaw and Rotterdam into surrender and attempted to repeat the tactics on London without success is today only a dying skeleton of its former self. By day and night American and RAF heavy bombers are carrying out long-range attacks over hundreds of miles of enemy territory and suffering only a small percentage lost, a percentage that grows smaller week by week.

The recent daytime attacks on German aircraft factories and assembly plants is being felt. Reports that considerable numbers of German night fighters are being put up day and night against the US bomber formations, probably indicate a shortage of day fighter aircraft, and that our system of 24-hour attacks is causing considerable fatigue to the Luftwaffe fighter pilots.

In the last three months of 1943, daylight bombers travelling across Germany frequently encountered the fighter rocket defences. Once the bombers got over their surprise they were able to take successful counter measures, and the success of their evasive tactics is shown by the fact that today the fighter rocket is not often seen. Among the new but unavailing forms of attack used by the German fighters is their use of cloud cover.

Friendly Enemies

A common practice of the Luftwaffe fighters is to join a bomber formation and to weave round them for often up to 20 minutes without making an attack. When they believe that the bombers have taken them as friendly fighters they make their attacks line abreast from the front, each fighter concentrating on one bomber.

By 1945 German air defences, regardless of how many anti-aircraft batteries, barrage balloons, radar facilities, or searchlight units there were, actually made that much of a difference regardless of where they were stationed, especially those tasked with defending towns and cities throughout Germany. This was not because the men operating them had suddenly become inept at their jobs, or because there had been a reduction in the production of equipment, although some units had been moved away from air defence duties in Germany to assist their comrades fighting the Soviet Union forces on the Eastern Front. It was because the British and

Americans had not only increased the number of bombing raids that they carried out, but had also increased the number of bombers that took part in each raid.

The edition of the *Manchester Evening News* of 26 February 1945, included an article under the heading:

Five German Flak Cars on One Train

Rocket typhoons of the RAF Second Tactical Air Force returned yesterday to the destruction, begun by the Tempests on Saturday, of a big German oil tank "farm" and installations near Hanover. Pilots found the ten great oil tanks still burning from the previous day's attack and a stream of black oil smoke stretching 20 miles towards Berlin. Typhoons poured 90 rockets into the central building. There was no flak and the gun emplacements were not even manned.

This was just a few months from the end of the war, when every soldier was a precious commodity for Adolf Hitler's quickly dwindling forces. Germany was being attacked on all sides by British, Commonwealth and American forces from the west and Russian forces from the east, all of which were heading for Berlin. Nazi Germany was almost in her final death throws, and simply didn't have the luxury of being able to have large numbers of its men manning anti-aircraft guns, which might manage to shoot down a few enemy aircraft, but they were not going to be able to stop the facilities that they were guarding from being bombed, so they could be better used elsewhere to protect their country. The article continued:

> *On the railways north and east of the Ruhr however, mobile flak was more intense than ever. Tempests encountered five flak cars on one track in the Brunswick area.*
>
> *"The flashes of flak just ripped from one end of the train to the other," said Flight-Lieut. R.J. Rothwell, of The Plantation, Aston, Nantwich, Cheshire, who brought a badly-holed Tempest back. Aircraft of the Second Tactical Air Force made 53 rail cuts and destroyed or damaged 88 locomotives, 201 rail trucks, 136 motor transport and 22 barges.*

It would appear that even when the German flak guns were manned, their effectiveness or their crews desire to fight was questionable. With the war drawing to an end most German soldiers would have known that it wasn't long before the war for them was lost. With that in mind, defending a by now worthless site or shooting down a few enemy aircraft had little relevance. The one thing left for them was to ensure they were captured by the British or American forces rather than the Russians.

On 2 March 1945 raids were carried out by aircraft of the USAAF against targets at Magdeburg, Chemnitz, and Dresden, along with two towns just south of Leipzig. More than 1,200 B-17 Flying Fortresses and Consolidated B-24

Liberators attacked synthetic oil plants at Magdeburg, Rositz and Bohlen, the large Krupp tank factory at Magdeburg, as well as the railyards at Chemnitz and Dresden. As if that wasn't enough for the German anti-aircraft batteries to contend with, the American bombers were escorted by more than 700 P-51 Mustang and P-47 Thunderbolt fighters.

The air raid on Dresden alone resulted in 940 tons of high-explosive bombs and 141 tons of incendiaries, being dropped on the city. It is hard to imagine what being on the receiving end of that amount of munitions could have felt like. Being a civilian would have been bad enough, but as a member of an anti-aircraft battery, a searchlight unit, or a radar technician, whose jobs meant that they were stationed either immediately on top of, or right next to a specific military target, must have been terrifying.

On the same night, Mosquito aircraft of the RAF's Bomber Command carried out an attack on Berlin and a communications centre at Erfurt in central Germany. Not one British aircraft failed to return to their home base after the raids. With Berlin being the nation's capital city, one would have expected it to have been heavily defended, which makes the fact that no British aircraft were shot down by anti-aircraft fire a staggering statistic.

What made a bad situation even worst for the German defenders was the introduction of British cluster bombs, which were said to have had a demoralising effect on German soldiers. Each bomb consisted of twenty-six smaller fragmentation bombs, each with its own parachute and timed to detonate just a short distance from the ground. A German Panzer Grenadier who had been captured by British forces, described them like this: *'They give you the creeps. They are worse than ordinary bombs, for they come from nowhere and the blast knocks you over before you know what has hit you.'*

The *Nottingham Journal* dated 11 June 1945, included an interesting article on the back page. A staff officer who had been an advisor to Air Chief Marshal Sir Arthur Harris during the Second World War, revealed a number of previously kept secrets in relation to what he referred to as the 'European War'. It came under the following heading:

Adviser to Harris on, 'How Bombers Did It'.

So confident were the Germans in 1939 and 1940, that the Reich would never be attacked, that the German Air Force had no night-fighter component, anti-aircraft guns being the only form of defence. It was only when the Battle of Britain failed that the Germans set aside some 250 Me.110s as a night fighter force. All German night-fighters throughout the war were converted bomber types, such as the Me. 110 and the Ju. 88 and the Do. 217.

The course of the battle is clearly revealed in Bomber Command casualties. In 1940 the loss was 1.6 p.c., in 1941 it was 2.5 p.c., then as the German defences got organised in 1942 it increased to 4 p.c., and in 1943 3.7 p.c. In 1944 air mastery began to assert itself and casualties dropped to 2.2 p.c., and in the five months of 1945 to 1.1 p.c.

It was found that German fighters converged on the RAF target areas arriving there in force about 20 minutes after the attack began. We even further concentrated our attacks, bringing in our bombers over the target at a rate of 1,800 an hour. No major attack lasted more than 20 minutes, so that our bombers were away before the fighters arrived.

The Germans then resorted to route interception, attacking the bombers as they crossed the coastline. By this time they had so increased the efficiency of their Radar that they knew when our bombers took off in Lincolnshire, Yorkshire and East Anglia. It was then that Bomber Command introduced feint attacks and night intruders.

Fortunately for Britain and her Allies Germany had unintentionally allowed herself to become complacent, especially throughout the first two years of the war, and her planning hadn't been all it should have been. As was said at the beginning of the article, Nazi Germany never really envisaged that she would find herself having to act in a defensive manner to any great degree, as she ran amok throughout Europe. She only saw a world where she would be the aggressor as she invaded and occupied country after country. Such an approach to warfare was always going to have repercussions, but Germany did not see that initially.

This meant that she spent a period of time having to play catch up, rather than having already stockpiled such defensive equipment prior to the outbreak of the war.

It wasn't until mid-1943 that Britain and America had amassed a sufficient number of four-engined bomber aircraft to be able to begin a sustained aerial assault on the heartland of Germany, targeting in particular the industrial areas which went a long way to feeding her war effort. Some members of the German hierarchy, such as Luftwaffe *Generalfeldmarschall* and convicted war criminal, Albert Kesselring and Field Marshal Karl Rudolf Gerd von Rundstedt, saw this as the beginning of the end for Germany, realising that it was a case of when, rather than if, they would lose the war.

Thursday, 22 February 1945 isn't a day that is marked by any particular celebration from an Allied perspective, but it should be, because as the *Western Daily Press* reported the following day, it was when some 6,000 Allied aircraft carried out a raid across the entirety of Hitler's breached and crumbling western line. This followed the previous day's night raid on Germany by 1,100 bomber aircraft of the RAF.

The 6,000 aircraft, which included those from America, Britain, Belgium, Italy and France, breached German air defences without too much trouble, carried out a plan which had been drawn up some months earlier, and in doing so struck a number of savage blows against Nazi Germany, stretching from Denmark to Austria and across the entire area of Central and Western Germany. The main aim of the raid was to disrupt and damage beyond repair the Reich's communication and transportation system, both railway and road, which was already under great strain due to the merciless damage caused by the almost continuous Allied air raids.

The raid began at 1pm and saw road and railway junctions, railway sidings and level crossings situated outside German towns and cities targeted with hundreds of thousands of bombs, rockets and cannon shells. What air defences Germany still had in place, when up against such numbers, would have stood little or no chance of even surviving the attack, let alone having the ability to make any impact in reducing the destructive nature of the Allied air raid. One thing for certain is that the air raid would have made any kind of transport impossible, which would have prevented Germany from being able to increase the size of its anti-aircraft batteries, search light units or barrage balloons. It would not have been possible to provide the anti-aircraft guns with ammunition and once they had run out, they could not fire their guns.

Here is a good example of how impossible a situation it had become for German air defences to have any real effect in carrying out their role. On 22 February 1945 some 1,000 bombers of the Fifteenth United States Army Air Force, operating out of bases in Italy, carried out raids on the Kempton railway yards on the Munich to Lake Constance line, the Rosenheim yards situated south east of Munich, and Altenmarkt, which is on the by-pass line which runs between Salzburg and Munich, as well as the Alpine rail network in Austria.

What was remarkable about these raids was the fact that this was the tenth consecutive day that these targets had been attacked by Allied aircraft. The chances are that by then there would have been very few, if any, anti-aircraft batteries left to defend the sites.

On 26 March 1948, one of the giant Flak towers which had been part of the city of Berlin's defensive anti-aircraft high rise platforms, was blown up and destroyed. Situated in the French sector of the city, the Flak tower was also home to an air-raid shelter which had been used on numerous occasions during the war. As if proof were needed of the Flak tower's strength, it took 50 tons of dynamite to finally turn it into a twisted mound of concrete, cement and steel. The once proud building was no more; the question is, why did it need to be destroyed? In the aftermath of the war, and with the rebuilding of the city still in its infancy, there was still a massive shortage of housing. Surely it could have been put to better use by providing much needed homes for some of the city's occupants. Sadly, the authorities had become concerned, paranoid even, that Nazi resistance groups might try and take the tower and use it as a stronghold. Although there was no intelligence to suggest that might be the case, the local authorities determined that as such a potential threat existed, the tower had to go. This was despite the fact that another of the Berlin Flak towers, in the Tiergarten, had been used as a hospital, and a similar structure in Vienna, Austria, had already been turned in to a hotel.

CHAPTER 11

Air Raids on German Cities

Once the Luftwaffe had realised the danger posed by the growing threat of the bombers of the RAF, they had to look to their home and make sure their own borders were as safe as they could be in the circumstances. With their usual efficiency, the Germans did not do things by half measures. They went about a massive expansion of their anti-aircraft capability. The number of personnel, both military and administrative, allocated to the organisation rose to over one million. The hardware and equipment put in place to protect Germany, and the occupied countries of which she had control, increased to 9,000 heavy artillery guns, 30,000 light guns and 15,000 heavy searchlights.

It is surprising that it was not already in place. This was after all the nation whose Nazi leaders had been planning for the Second World War since they came into power in 1933, and only began their attacks on Czechoslovakia and Poland when they felt that they were fully prepared. It is inconceivable to think that they could not have considered a scenario that would not have resulted in German soil being attacked from the air.

When Air Chief Marshal Sir Arthur Harris was put in charge of Bomber Command he said:

> *The Nazis entered this war under the rather childish delusion that they were going to bomb everyone else, and nobody was going to bomb them. At Rotterdam, London, Warsaw, and half a hundred other places, they put their rather naïve theory into operation. They sowed the wind, and now they are going to reap the whirlwind.*

By the end of the war Germany had been bombed to pieces. Allied aircraft dropped more than one million tons of bombs on Germany, which resulted in more than a million civilian casualties, of whom some 300,000 were killed. In the beginning, Germany possibly felt that her Luftwaffe fighters were invincible, a claim they could have fairly made in the early stages of the war.

Under Harris's command things didn't always go his way. To start with the number of aircraft that were sent on bombing missions was recognised as being insufficient, for a number of reasons. Partly this was down to inadequate navigation, some of it was because of inaccurate bombing, but most of it was because of the effectiveness of the defences they came up against, both the fighter aircraft in the skies and the accuracy of the anti-aircraft batteries on the ground. Undeterred, Harris pressed for air raids on a much larger scale, which would remove the effectiveness of anti-aircraft batteries from the equation. He got his way with Operation Millennium, which was the first 'thousand-bomber raid' on the German city of Cologne on the night of 30/31 May 1942.

The operation had two main goals, although the first one was more of a hope. The devastation of the raid was expected to be so great that it would be sufficient to knock Germany out of the war, or at least severely damage German civilian morale. Secondly, was the propaganda aspect both for the Allies and Harris's concept of a strategic bombing offensive. Not everybody in government was totally convinced or comfortable with the aerial tactics Harris deployed, but he knew a successful raid on a German city would go a long way to convincing the War Cabinet to support Bomber Command and provide it with the men and equipment which it needed to move forward, and play an important part in bringing the war to an early conclusion.

Harris managed to find enough men and equipment to send a total of 1,047 bombers on the raid on Cologne. He also sent 113 other aircraft on a diversionary raid to harass German night fighter airfields as well as keeping anti-aircraft batteries occupied. By the time the raid was over, the effectiveness – or the non-effectiveness – of anti-aircraft batteries had been laid bare. Out of the 1,047 bombers sent on the raid, 43 were lost and only 16 of these had been brought down by anti-aircraft fire. Ironically, of over 100 public buildings that were damaged or destroyed in the raid, only one of them was of a military nature and that was the Flak barracks that housed the anti-aircraft battery crews.

Most of the damage caused was to civilian housing, the very people and properties that the anti-aircraft batteries were in place to protect. Some 13,000 were destroyed outright, just over 6,000 were seriously damaged, and 22,270 were slightly damaged, such as having windows smashed or tiles knocked off of the roof.

One of the British bombers that was brought down by the anti-aircraft flak batteries was an Avro 679 Manchester twin engine medium bomber. The captain and pilot of the aircraft was Leslie Thomas Manser. As Manser flew in over the target at just over 7,000 feet, his aircraft was caught in the beams of the searchlights and made him an easy target for the anti-aircraft units. In no time at all the ground batteries had done their job and Manser's aircraft was hit by Flak, although by taking evasive action he managed to escape from the beams and Flak and make good his escape. With his rear gunner wounded, his cockpit filling up with smoke, and his port engine over-heating, he was in a bad way. But rather than abandon the aircraft and risk being captured, Manser tried to get his aircraft and crew to safety. For a while the crippled aircraft was limping along, but then disaster struck: the port engine burst into flames, which slowed the aircraft down causing it to lose height. With the aircraft now over Belgium, and a crash now almost inevitable, Manser ordered his crew to bail out, and to ensure that they could all parachute out safely he remained at the controls. The aircraft crashed into a dyke at Bree, near Genk in Belgium, and burst into flames. Four of the five crew who parachuted to safety made it back home to England, whilst the fifth was captured by the Germans. Manser was buried at the Heverlee War Cemetery in Leuven, Belgium. For his actions that evening, Manser was posthumously awarded the Victoria Cross.

Little did the crew of an anti-aircraft battery located in Cologne realise that their dogged determination to protect the city would result in a British bomber aircraft crashing in another country.

In another twist of fate Manser's brother-in-law, Captain John Neil Randle, serving with 'B' Company, 2nd Battalion, Royal Norfolk Regiment, was also posthumously awarded the Victoria Cross in 1944, during the Battle of Khomina in North East India against the Japanese.

The 'thousand-bomber raid' over Cologne was deemed to be a success, which it definitely was for the British, but for the Germans it highlighted just how ineffective their anti-aircraft batteries were against an air raid that involved a large number of enemy aircraft. In addition, it is worth noting that between 13 February 1940 and 2 March 1945, Cologne was bombed on 260 separate occasions, which means the city was attacked, on average, once every four days. During those raids, an estimated 20,000 people were killed.

Putting into perspective the pressure that Germany's anti-aircraft units were under to protect installations, factories, homes, and cities throughout the country, on the evening of 5/6 March 1943, 442 aircraft from Bomber Command carried out their 100,000th sortie of the war, when the

Krupps factory at Essen was bombed, destroying fifty-three of its buildings. This was also the first raid of the Battle of the Ruhr, which lasted for five months. Despite the aircraft involved being equipped with the Oboe blind bombing system, which marked the point of the intended attack using radio transponder technology and linked equipment on the aircraft with radio transmitters on the ground, only 153 of the attacking aircraft dropped their bombs within 3 miles of the aiming point. Fourteen aircraft were lost in the raid, most of which were brought down by anti-aircraft batteries.

Between 12 March and 13 June 1943, the following thirteen raids by Bomber Command took place as part of the Battle of the Ruhr; there were others, but these highlight the almost impossible task that the German air defences faced.

On 12/13 March, just one week after the Krupps factory in Essen had been attacked by 442 aircraft, it was attacked again, this time by 457 aircraft, including Lancasters, Wellingtons, Halifaxes, Stirlings and Mosquitos. Despite the anti-aircraft batteries' best efforts, they only managed to shoot down 23 of the bombers, which is about 5 per cent, meaning that 434 managed to get through and drop their bombs.

On 3/4 April Essen was bombed yet again, but this time a staggering 797 aircraft from Bomber Command were used in the raid.

On 8/9 April Duisburg was the target and was attacked by 392 aircraft. The German air defence anti-aircraft batteries managed to shoot down 19 of the bombers, once again, roughly 5 per cent of the aircraft involved in the air raid. This was a figure that was considered to be an acceptable loss by the British military authorities.

On 26/27 April Duisburg was the target again, this time by 561 aircraft, 17 of which were brought down by the anti-aircraft batteries, roughly 3 per cent of the aircraft involved in the raid. Once again, this fell into the acceptable losses category for Bomber Command.

On 30 April/1 May it was Essen's turn, which was attacked by 305 aircraft.

On 4/5 May 596 aircraft carried out an attack on the German city of Dortmund.

On 13/14 May Bochum was the next German city to be attacked, this time by 442 aircraft of Bomber Command. Many of the bombs were dropped harmlessly off target, due to the effective German use of decoy markers. The RAF lost 24 of its aircraft, which is 6 per cent of the total number.

On 16/17 May a raid that has gone down in British military history proving the fact that 'necessity is the mother of invention' took place. This was the night that saw the Barnes Wallis's 'bouncing bomb' in use by No.617 Squadron of the RAF's Bomber Command. Nineteen of the squadron's aircraft attacked the Möhne, Edersee and the Sorpe dams in Operation Chastise. The first two dams were breached, but the Sorpe Dan sustained only minor damage. The raid caused catastrophic flooding of the Ruhr valley and the villages located in the Eder valley. Sadly, it is estimated that 1,600 civilians lost their lives, 600 of whom were Germans, with most of the remaining 1,000 being Russian forced labourers, who were probably captured soldiers. The raid also saw the destruction of two hydroelectric power stations, with several others sustaining damage.

The Germans knew the importance of the dams not only to themselves but to the Allies in being able to attack them. Accordingly, they were defended by a total of six light 20mm Flak guns, one on each of the towers at either side of the dam. One was on the dam wall itself, and three more below the dam wall, protecting the power station. The German soldiers who were manning the guns at the Möhne dam were from the 3rd Light Flak battery 840, which was a unit of the Flak-Regiment 124. Between them they shot down eight of the RAF aircraft, killing 53 of the aircrew, with another three who were captured and taken as prisoners of war. This means that approximately 45 per cent of the aircraft on the raid did not make it back home, and with 53 of the 133 crew who took part in the raid being killed, this meant that nearly 40 per cent of the crews were lost as well. This is a good example of how the percentage of aircraft lost in such raids was dependant on how many took part; the more that took part, the lower the percentage of aircraft and airmen lost.

Wing Commander Guy Gibson, aged 24, who led the attack on the Möhne dam, was awarded the Victoria Cross. It was a very daring and dangerous raid, as because of the 'bouncing' bombs being used, the attacking aircraft had to come in on the dams at a height of no more than 100 feet. No.617 Squadron were for ever more known as the 'Dam Busters'.

On 23/24 May 826 aircraft of Bomber Command carried out an attack on Dortmund, where they dropped 2,000 tons of heavy explosive and incendiary bombs in just one hour. As a result of the attack, the Hoesch steelworks ceased production, but the RAF did not get it all its own way, as 35 of its aircraft were shot down by the city's anti-aircraft units.

On 25/26 May 729 aircraft attacked the German city of Düsseldorf, but due to heavy cloud and decoy fires, the RAF's bombing was mostly off target. They also lost 26 of their aircraft, shot down by the German ground defences.

On 27/28 May Essen was once again attacked by the RAF. This time by 518 aircraft with 23 of them being brought down during the raid.

On 29/30 May 719 bombers attacked Wuppertal. Five out of the city's six major factories were destroyed, along with 100,000 homes. Most of the old town was built out of wood and burnt so fiercely that it caused a fire storm.

On 11/12 June Düsseldorf was again attacked by 783 aircraft when German anti-aircraft units shot down 38 aircraft.

On 12/13 June it was Bochum again when 503 RAF bombers carried out an attack on the city, but strong German defences saw 24 British aircraft shot down.

These raids show that despite being up against ridiculous odds, the German anti-aircraft batteries did not give up, but carried on regardless of what was thrown at them. What the men who operated the guns must have thought when they looked up to the skies and heard the combined noise of hundreds of incoming RAF bombers is hard to imagine. They must have been very brave men to have done what they did and stayed at their post whilst bombs were dropping all around them. The cacophony of ear drum shattering noise mixed in with the fear, panic and sheer adrenalin rush of the situation, must have been emotionally draining for all concerned, but despite this they did their jobs, downing many Allied aircraft in the process.

As the war continued and the Luftwaffe became less effective, the German homeland became more and more dependent on its anti-aircraft batteries to protect them from the incessant threat of Allied bombers. With some of the raids in the latter part of the war consisting of more than 1,000 aircraft, the Luftwaffe simply did not have anywhere near the required number of anti-aircraft batteries to prevent their cities from being devastated and destroyed, or their citizens killed in their thousands. But with the decline in its air superiority, Nazi Germany had to find another way of preventing the wholesale destruction of its homeland by Allied bombing missions on its major towns and cities.

The only way to try and combat this ever-increasing Allied threat was by increasing its Flak forces and anti-aircraft batteries, as the responsibility for home air defence now lay with them. To this end German cities such as Berlin, Hamburg, Dresden, Munich, Dortmund and Frankfurt saw a dramatic increase in the number of anti-aircraft batteries springing up all over the place, especially around landmarks which had been designated or identified as being key targets for American and British bombers.

Before January 1944, German fighters had been the key defensive enforcer, responsible for shooting down the American bombers, such as the B-17 Flying Fortress. Within five months all of that had changed. By June 1944 the Luftwaffe's power in the skies had waned dramatically and they were responsible for shooting down only 80 American bombers, whilst during that time frame the anti-aircraft units accounted for 201.

CHAPTER 12

Press Reports of German Air Defences

The fate of Germany had been sealed when Adolf Hitler was made Chancellor of Germany on 30 January 1933, by President Paul von Hindenburg. This was a decision Hindenburg made reluctantly, and purely for political reasons. It is also a decision would regret, and one for which the German people would pay a very high price.

What was noticeable were the number of articles which appeared in British newspapers concerning the topic of German air defences.

On 19 October 1933, Count Schwerin von Krosigk, Germany's Minister of Finance, made an announcement in relation to the aerial defence of his nation in the case of an emergency. It concerned all monies that had been expended by individuals or firms for the advancement of Germany's protection from air attacks, and which could be deducted in total from their income or corporation tax returns.

By the Treaty of Versailles, Germany was forbidden military planes. We are denied, therefore the most effective weapon against air attacks. All the greater importance, therefore attaches to the civil air protection measures calculated to safeguard the population against danger from the air. In the interests of the population, as well as of national defence, such measures must, therefore, be widely encouraged by a policy of tax deduction.

The air protection measures mainly concerned major industrial premises, where large numbers of employees worked, although it also included homes. The Count also touched on the topic of the building of gas and bomb proof cellars, the purchase of gasmasks and making arrangements for the installation of alarms, as well as drilling special units in the use of such defensive equipment.

On 17 April 1934, the following article appeared in the *Sunderland Daily Echo and Shipping Gazette*:

The German Note explaining the reasons for the increased estimates for national defence in reality adds very little to the facts which were known in this country. There is greater detail and the statement of the German Foreign Minister, indicates that the 50 per cent increase in naval estimates is due to the need for renovation of obsolete units. The military changes, namely, the conversion of the long service Army into a more numerous force of short service

men, was a provision urged upon Germany by the
Disarmament Conference, therefore no criticism
can be directed to this change.

Regardless of that opinion, the trebling of estimates for
their air services and defences was a big indicator of a
determination to greatly increase her air defences against
the perceived threat of an attack or invasion from the
air by an unknown or even non-existent enemy. Despite
these measures being undertaken by Germany, it did not
really sound any alarm bells about where this was leading.
Even when it was reported that Germany had begun a
programme to build splinter and gas proof cellars, with
selected individuals being trained in poison gas defensive
measures, the strongest words of concern were: *'Such*
steps are typical of traditional German thoroughness and
organisation.'

Was it right that Germany should have spent such
large sums of money on defensive measures against what
the rest of the world, not realising what was going to take
place, would have seen as an imaginary danger or threat?
By then Germany was struggling to meet its foreign debt,
which had been placed upon her by the Treaty of Versailles
at the end of the First World War. The nation's levels of
unemployment were increasing, yet on the international
stage nobody seemed to question the large sums of money
she was spending on defence.

Although it could be argued that what was happening in
Germany was a matter for the German people, it had unknown

repercussions on the wider international community, at a time where the memory of the death and destruction of the First World War was still fresh in people's minds. This was also a time where the talk was of disarmament, not of stockpiling military hardware. The obvious question to ask must have been what spending limit, if any, was Germany placing upon herself in relation to her defensive measures and were the massive sums of money she was spending just a beginning? Germany had called for an equality of armaments, if this was an unobtainable concession from the international community, ensuring her nation's safety and sovereignty was obviously the next best thing.

Looking back at this scenario with the benefit of hindsight, how Germany's build-up of her defensive capabilities did not start alarm bells ringing amongst other nations is hard to fathom. It must have been clear that none of her neighbouring countries would try to invade her for any territorial gain, she had not been threatened by any of them, so why the need for such large-scale defensive capabilities? No other European nation had thought to make such increases in their air defensive capabilities or had anywhere near the same capability.

On 12 January 1938, just twenty months from the outbreak of the Second World War, it was announced by the Home Office that the Parliamentary Under Secretary at the Home Office, Mr Geoffrey Lloyd, would be visiting Berlin the following week. The purpose of his visit was to study certain points in German air raid precautions. Nazi Germany had previously allowed visits from officials from

Britain's Air Raids Precautions Department. What had prompted this visit was unknown, but it was clear that the real reason behind why Germany had invested so heavily in her defences was still unknown to Britain and her Allies.

Although Germany was telling everybody who cared to listen that her programme of building bunkers and cellars and updating her air defences was purely for defensive reasons in the case of attack, there may have been a different explanation. Many of these air defences and bunker systems had been put in place close to premises with large work forces. These same premises were where military hardware such as tanks, artillery pieces and aircraft were being built in direct breach of the Treaty of Versailles. Having undertaken such a programme of defiance they needed to be able to protect their operation. Nobody had worked out why Germany should have any such fear of an air attack. The reality was that if any of the nations discovered what she was really up to, especially those who had been enemies during the First World War, and a signatory to the Treaty of Versailles, the chances are they would have looked to have carried out air attacks on these very premises.

On 11 July 1939, with the war still some two months away, Britain stretched her protective wings over France, in the shape of a training flight. Twelve squadrons of RAF bombers made non-stop flights by arrangement of the French Air Ministry. More than 100 aircraft and 400 crew members took part. They covered some 120,000 miles at a pre-agreed cruising height and speed, making sure that they stayed well away from any of Germany's borders.

On 7 September 1939 a brief resumé of the war to that date included comments about the RAF and Germany's air defence given by Prime Minister Neville Chamberlain in the House of Commons. In his review of these early events he paid a well-deserved tribute to the courage and skill of the nation's airmen, who had bombed the German Fleet at their bases at Wilhelmshaven, where one of the German pocket battleships was hit twice by bombs dropped by the RAF. The Kiel Canal and the German naval bases were perhaps the most strongly fortified places in Germany and when the aircraft of the RAF carried out their attack, the weather was inclement, with poor visibility and what was described as 'a blinding rainstorm'.

British air crews had carried out four reconnaissance flights over Germany and, besides gathering valuable information, they also dropped millions of leaflets printed in German containing propaganda which was intended to influence the German people against their Nazi leaders. There was a belief amongst British intelligence officers that the war was far from being popular with large sections of the German population. It was further reported that there was actual discord among German soldiers stationed along the Siegfried Line, but it was debatable how much truth there was in that statement.

It was encouraging to know that the German air defences could be successfully penetrated, and although they were in full operation, they did not manage to shoot down a single aircraft.

On 10 October 1939, just over a month into the war, it was announced that British aircraft had carried out a reconnaissance flight along the entire German frontier, stretching from France to the North Sea. The aircraft were initially sent to investigate reports of the evacuation of important cities, and big troop movements near Aix-la-Chapelle, a spa and border city in the North Rhine-Westphalia region of Germany. There were also reports of what had been described as a 'significant concentration' of aircraft and an intensive building of military fortifications along Germany's border with Luxembourg.

RAF aircraft took a large number of photographs of the enemy positions they flew over, which were examined on their return by experts from British Military Intelligence. They had flown in pairs from an unspecified aerodrome somewhere behind the Maginot Line. Due to bad weather that two of the aircraft ran in to, they were forced to fly for most of the time at just over 6,000 feet. As they passed the southernmost tip of Luxembourg, French artillery units were firing on the Siegfried Line, immediately below where they were flying, but undeterred they continued their observations, dodging from one gap in the clouds to another.

As they reached the German city of Koblenz, on the banks of the Rhine where it is joined by the Moselle, anti-aircraft units opened fire on them, although hidden by the clouds, the sound of their engines would have been impossible to hide. In the circumstances the best that the German gunners could do was to try to judge the range and direction by the sound of the aircraft's engines. Although the shells screamed up through the clouds and burst all around them, none of the planes were hit and continued on their way.

Having been detected by the German anti-aircraft units, their presence in the area was no longer a secret, and the units at Koblenz must have telephoned ahead because by the time the British aircraft had reached Siegburg, they came under immediate attack from anti-aircraft units. Once again the outcome was the same, and they passed on slightly shaken but unscathed. In no time at all they saw the Rhine, turned west and disappeared into Holland, where the low cloud base and inclement weather made it impossible for them to see anything else, without the risk of flying too low and making themselves susceptible to ground fire from German anti-aircraft units. They flew on to the North Sea coast of Germany, turned left and headed for home, which was an airfield somewhere along the south coast of England, where intelligence experts were waiting to develop and examine the photographs they had taken.

The three pairs of aircraft had taken off at different times to ensure that between them they would be able to take all of the photographs that were needed to build a complete picture of Germany's air defences which had been put in place along her borders. All six of the aircraft completed their mission and made it safely back to England.

Speaking on Berlin wireless on 31 January 1941, the German Air Secretary of State and the Inspector General of the German Air Force, General Erhard Milch, exhorted the German people not to expect miracles from the German anti-aircraft defences, adding that in modern warfare attacks were not only directed against the enemy on the battlefield, but also against the nerve of the civilian.

Describing the difficulties confronting the German anti-aircraft defences, Milch added that British aircraft were entering Germany at great heights. It was impossible to see which way they were going to fly. He added that the air raid alarm is sounded regardless of whether bombs were dropped or not, as it was not possible to know if the aircraft were flying over en route to another destination or were about to drop bombs where they were. If they waited to sound the alarm, it could then be too late. Regarding when it was appropriate to give the all-clear, Milch said that was a difficult decision as if given too early the aircraft could just as easily turn round and drop their bombs.

Many people had asked him how it was possible that the RAF and Americans were able to penetrate so far into Germany, and when they attempted to, why the anti-aircraft defences did not prevent the enemy from entering Germany. He re-iterated that it was difficult but pointed out that because of the skill of the anti-aircraft batteries, British day time raids were nearly unheard of, but despite this attacking aircraft would always hold an advantage over anti-aircraft units.

Milch ended by saying that incessant work was going on to find a satisfactory solution to deal with incidents, however his ineffective management resulted in the decline of the German Luftwaffe and its loss of air superiority. After the war he was arrested and tried at Nuremberg and found guilty on two counts. Firstly, for war crimes and secondly crimes against humanity. He was sentenced to life imprisonment at Landsberg prison, but in 1951 this was reduced to fifteen years imprisonment. He was released in 1954, having served just seven years. He lived out the rest of his life in Düssledorf, where he died in 1972. There had been rumours circulating for years that his father, a pharmacist Anton Milch, was in fact Jewish. Luckily for him he had the support of Herman Göring, who had the investigation by the SS into the matter, halted.

In February 1942 it was acknowledged by RAF pilots that attempting to successfully pierce through German air defences over Germany was no mean feat. They had improved greatly from what they had been at the beginning of the war even though they had been developing their defences from soon after Hitler had become the German Chancellor in 1933. The aircrews flying into Germany found the flak fire from anti-aircraft batteries both fierce and accurate. The heavy ground fire that RAF crews had to endure made it extremely difficult for them to reach their objectives and then carry out their attacks effectively. As if that was not bad enough, they then had to turn round and fly back through the same accurate flak fire to get back home to their base. The German air defences had reached such a level of effectiveness by early 1942 that even when British bombers did manage to get through to their targets, they were not always accurate and therefore failed to have as big an impact as they wanted on reducing German industrial output.

Another interesting factor of air raids by the RAF on German cities was the differing reports that both sides released. On the evening of 31 August 1943, Bomber Command carried out an air raid on Berlin. The following is a communiqué that was issued by the Air Ministry the following day:

Last night a great weight of high explosive and incendiary bombs were dropped on Berlin in 45 minutes. Broken clouds at low levels made it difficult to assess results visually, but large fires were seen, and the indications are that great damage was done. The enemy put up very large fighter forces over the capital and its approaches, in an unsuccessful attempt to prevent the launching of a concentrated attack. A number of his aircraft were destroyed in combat.

Airfields and other targets in France and the Low Countries were also attacked during the night. Forty-seven bombers and one fighter are missing. Throughout the night the roar of planes, including heavy bombers, going to the continent, was almost incessant. For upwards of two hours before daybreak our bombers were streaming back across the Channel. From time to time ack-ack gun fire was seen bursting over the French coast at Boulogne and Calais. Streams of tracers were also sent up by the enemy defences. Once again the Germans state that it was a "terror raid" and claim that a considerable number of bombers were shot down.

Here is the German version of the same raid as released by the German News Agency:

Last night a new British terror raid was made on Berlin. Newly reorganised German air defences inflicted extremely heavy losses on the raiders. The British bomber formations were dispersed and forced to jettison most of their bombs. Thanks to the efficient defence, the concentrated attack by the British bombers was frustrated. Above and below the clouds, heavy air combats developed, in the course of which numerous British bombers were shot down. The total of British losses cannot yet be estimated. It is already certain however, that the German air defences, flak and night fighters alike, have inflicted very heavy losses on the RAF.

The news agency later claimed that more than 30 British bombers were shot down. Besides the agency's report, there was also an official German communiqué of the same incident:

Last night strong British air formations again attacked the area of Greater Berlin. Our night bombers, in co-operation with anti-aircraft and searchlight batteries, disturbed the enemy bomber formations and the intended concentrated effect of the raid was thwarted. In some districts of the city and in the vicinity of the capital, damage was caused, some of it considerable. The population suffered slight casualties. Enemy nuisance raiders flying singly, also dropped bombs at random, on some places in Germany.

Air defence forces brought down 47 British bombers, according to reports so far to hand. Eight more planes were lost by the enemy over the occupied territories in the west yesterday.

The number of British bombers brought down was agreed as being 47, but this may have been a case of the official German communiqué using the same number as had been reported by the Air Ministry the previous day.

By January 1944 Germany was being bombed remorselessly by Bomber Command and the United States Air Force, which was placing an unrealistic challenge on the shoulders of those responsible for the country's air defence units. The Air Ministry announced that on the evening of 14 January 1944, aircraft from the RAF's No.106 Squadron, which was part of No.5 Group, Bomber Command, carried out air raids on Braunschweig, Magdeburg and Berlin, as part of Operation Hurricane, the intention of which was to demonstrate the capabilities of Allied bombing.

Braunschweig, a city in Lower Saxony and an important centre of Germany's aircraft and engineering industry, had 2,000 bombs dropped on it alone, leaving large areas of the city on fire for nearly three days. This wasn't the first attempt to inflict lasting damage on Braunschweig during

1944. There had been four previous attempts, but each one had failed due to a combination of inclement weather and strong German defences, including anti-aircraft batteries situated in and around the city. On more than one occasion these batteries had won the day, proving their effectiveness in the battle for the skies.

The orders for the operation included the following:

> *In order to demonstrate to the enemy in Germany generally, the overwhelming superiority of the Allied Air Forces in this theatre…. the intention is to apply within the shortest period the maximum effort of the Royal Air Force Bomber Command and the Eighth United States Bomber Command against objectives in the densely populated Ruhr.*

Operation Hurricane saw 1,000 RAF bombers head for the Rhineland city of Duisburg, along with 1,200 bombers of the USAAF, whilst a further 233 RAF bombers were allocated to attack Braunschweig, whose population at the time was 150,000. By the end of the war, Braunschweig had been the subject of forty-two air raids, even though Bomber Command knew that the city was surrounded by anti-aircraft units. It also had six extremely large underground bunkers and two air raid shelters. They were so big in fact that some 23,000 people had sought refuge in them, but as the firestorm caused by the bombing took hold, danger lurked for those inside, as the fear was that they would suffocate. Those in the bunkers were saved, but at one of the city's air raid shelters, 95 out of 104 people were killed when they suffocated, so intense was the fire storm.

Two points worth highlighting here are that the number of civilians who perished that night has been debated for years, with figures varying between 484 and over 1,000. If it hadn't been for the local fire brigade who rescued the 23,000 holed up in the bunkers, the casualty figures would have been much higher.

Of the 233 aircraft of Bomber Command which attacked Braunschweig on 14 October 1944, only one Lancaster was brought down as a result of anti-aircraft fire, despite the fact that the city had a ring of anti-aircraft batteries spread out around it. The attack on Braunschweig proved just how difficult it was for the anti-aircraft batteries to be really effective against large scale bombing raids, especially night-time ones. If an aircraft was caught in the beam of a spotlight then the gunners on the anti-aircraft batteries had half a chance at downing the aircraft, but if they couldn't see them, all they could do was aim towards the noise of the aircraft's engines.

This was the beginning of four days of daytime attacks by aircraft of the RAF's VIII Air Force of Bomber Command, flying out of England, and elements of the Fifteenth USAAF, taking off from an air base in Italy, on locations across Germany and Austria.

The first target was the German aircraft factories at Gotha, and the ball-bearing factory at Schweinfurt, which was attacked by the RAF, along with the German aircraft factory at Steyr in Austria, which was attacked by aircraft of the USAAF. American Flying Fortresses also successfully attacked the Daimler factory at Stuttgart, which produced engines for tanks, submarines, aircraft, as well as barrels for the Mauser military rifle. By the end of the raid the entire factory was ablaze, which was confirmed by reconnaissance photographs taken at the time. It had not been an easy raid for the B-17 Flying Fortresses to carry out. Escorted as they were by Thunderbolt and Lightning fighters, they were met some 18 miles away from their intended target by around 100 German fighters, who quickly swarmed round the Fortresses and the battle commenced. It continued until all the American aircraft had completed their bombing runs.

The United States Eighth Army Air Force lost 49 of its aircraft on the mission, and with ten men to each aircraft, that is nearly 500 men. How many were shot down by German aircraft or by the ground based anti-aircraft batteries, was not clarified. How many of the aircraft crash-landed or how many men managed to parachute out of them and survived, is not known. The escorting aircraft for the Flying Fortresses, which came from the RAF, the Eighth and Ninth American Air Force Groups, as well as Dominion aircraft, managed to shoot down 37 of the German fighters. Ten of the Allied fighters did not return to their base.

The German News Agency stated that German air defences were in action all over the northern and southern areas of the Reich and dealt with those aircraft who carried out the attacks as well as those who were flying over southern Germany with fighter escorts, but only acting as a diversion.

CHAPTER 13

German Aircraft Production

Effective air defences do not just mean anti-aircraft batteries and searchlight units on the ground, but also an effective air service. In a large bomber raid over Germany, fighter aircraft also played their part in disrupting and shooting down Britain's bombers. From a defensive perspective, having an effective air force was of primary importance. If a country had that, it made life easier for the gun batteries on the ground.

Throughout the war, Germany had the second worst aircraft production figures, coming fourth out of five nations. Although somewhat ironically, her aircraft production figures rose year on year between 1939 and 1944, culminating in the last year at 40,593, this figure dropped to 7,540 in 1945. The problem for Germany was not necessarily the numbers of aircraft that she was producing, rather the amount she was losing. The more aircraft lost, the more experienced pilots lost as well, and it was the experience of these men that it was hard to replace.

Germany built fifteen different types of fighter aircraft during the war, the main weapon of choice used to attack Allied bombers en route to Germany to bomb her cities and large industrial areas. The five main types were Dornier, Focke-Wulf, Heinkel, Junkers, and Messerschmitt. Production figures show that she focused on two main aircraft: the Messerschmitt Bf 109, of which 29,155 were built, and the Focke-Wulf Fw 190, of which 13,376 were built. These two aircraft were way ahead of any others that Nazi Germany produced throughout the war.

It is clear to see that by 1945, Germany's aircraft production had almost come to a grinding halt. This shortage would have had a major knock-on effect to the anti-aircraft batteries, whose workload would have dramatically increased, especially as the number of bombers that Britain and America were sending across the English Channel to attack her cities was becoming larger and larger.

CHAPTER 14

The Bombing of Dresden

It would be remiss not to include a chapter about the Allied bombing of Dresden between 13 and 15 February 1945, as it highlights the dire straits that Germany was in at that time of the war. The Luftwaffe could only muster a total of 28 Messerschmidt Bf 110s in the defence of Dresden, which spoke volumes about how low Germany had fallen from her heyday in the early stages of the war. The second point is that the Allies sent a combined total of 2,080 bomber and fighter aircraft on the raid, and only seven of them did not make it back, which suggests that anti-aircraft cover for the city was almost non-existent. In fact, Dresden's anti-aircraft guns had been removed to help in the fight against the Red Army, with the last heavy Flak battery having been removed in January 1945. The main reason for there being so few aircraft to effectively challenge the RAF and USAAF in the skies over Dresden was down to a lack of pilots and a shortage of aviation fuel. The city's radar system had also been downgraded, which meant that the time defensive units had to prepare for raid was greatly reduced.

Of the seven Allied bombers lost during the raid, six were from the RAF and one was from the USAAF. Three of the British bombers were lost when they were hit by bombs dropped by other British aircraft flying above them.

The bombing of Dresden took place over three days, came in the shape of four raids, and was a combined Allied effort between Britain and America. The RAF sent over 769 heavy bombers on the raid, and the USAAF 527 of their heavy bombers, along with 784 P-51 Mustang fighter aircraft, which were acting as escort cover for the bombers. Between them they dropped a total of 3,900 tons of high explosive bombs and incendiary devices, which resulted in a firestorm that destroyed large areas of the city. Estimates of civilian casualties vary. Just after the raids it was said that up to 25,000 people had been killed, although these casualty figures have been studied over the years and it would fair to say that there is still disagreement concerning how many were actually killed. Some of this confusion on the matter came about as a result of German refugees who were also in the city, having fled westwards from ever-advancing Russian forces.

The rights and wrongs of the raid have been discussed time and again over the years, with some saying that Dresden was a legitimate and strategic target, as it was a major railway hub, communication centre, and had more than 100 factories that produced materials and items for Germany's war effort. Between them they had a workforce of more than 50,000.

The question has always been 'why Dresden?' as it had little or no strategic purpose, especially so late in the war. It would appear that the raids were better described as being totally indiscriminate rather than having specifically targeted buildings with any military or government connection.

Sadly, there were not many air raid shelters in Dresden. The main one was at the city's railway station, which could house more than 6,000 people. In the subsequent fire storm that followed, large parts of the city were engulfed in flames, which was made worst by the wooden structure of many of the buildings. One such area was the old section of the town, and what was known as the inner eastern suburbs. Almost 12,000 homes were destroyed along with countless shops, warehouses, theatres, cultural buildings, government buildings, schools, hospitals, the Zoo, the city's railway, factories, engineering works, and even ships and barges. Across the city it is estimated that the raids on Dresden resulted in more than 100,000 dwellings being either completely destroyed or left uninhabitable.

The bombing of Dresden was for some 'a bridge too far'. In the minds of many, it had over-stepped the bounds of common decency, regardless of being at war with an enemy state. Although a lot of the subsequent attitudes towards what had happened at Dresden had been shaped by what the Nazi Propaganda Ministry of Joseph Goebbels had told the world, many had jumped on it as being the absolute and utter truth, which had then shaped their views and opinions, although they were based in part on fiction.

Winston Churchill, who had never been totally convinced by the tactics of Bomber Command, was quick to distance himself from the bombing of Dresden.

It seems to me that the moment has come when the question of bombing German cities simply for the sake of increasing the terror, though under other pretexts, should be reviewed. Otherwise we shall come into control of an utterly ruined land.…. The destruction of Dresden remains a serious query against the conduct of Allied bombing. I am of the opinion that military objectives must henceforward be more strictly studied in our own interests than that of the enemy.

The Foreign Secretary has spoken to me on this subject, and I feel the need for more precise concentration upon military objectives such as oil and communications behind the immediate battle zone, rather than on mere acts of terror and wanton destruction, however impressive.

On having been shown a paraphrased version of Churchill's memo, Air Chief Marshal Arthur 'Bomber' Harris wrote the following to the Air Ministry:

I assume the view under consideration is something like this: no doubt in the past we were justified in attacking German cities. But to do so was always repugnant and now the Germans are beaten anyway we can properly abstain from proceeding with these attacks. This is a doctrine to which I could never subscribe. Attacks on cities like any other act of war are intolerable unless they are strategically justified.

But they are strategically justified in so far as they tend to shorten the war and preserve the lives of Allied soldiers. To my mind we have obviously no right to give them up unless it is certain that they will not have this effect. I do not personally regard the whole of the remaining cities of Germany as worth the bones of one British Grenadier.

The feeling, such as there is, over Dresden, could be easily explained by any psychiatrist. It is connected with German bands and Dresden shepherdesses. Actually, Dresden was a mass of munitions works, an intact government centre, and a key transportation point to the east. It is now none of these things.

It was clear that Arthur Harris was not a man for bending. His view on the RAF's part throughout the entire war was that the strategy of carrying out bombing raids on enemy locations, no matter where they were, was the right and proper thing to do – because he was a warmonger, but because he was a patriot who genuinely saw it as a way to bring the war to an expedient end, which ultimately helped save British and Allied lives.

The Chief of the Air Staff, Sir Charles Portal, along with Arthur Harris, was not at all impressed with the content of Churchill's memo, especially the phrase, 'acts of terror', so under pressure from the Chiefs of Staff, and because of the annoyance caused to Portal and Harris, Churchill, re-worded his memo slightly, leaving out the offending phrase.

If Germany had won the war, it is possible that the bombing of Dresden would have been treated by the Nazi Party as a war crime, and those responsible would have been brought to justice.

CHAPTER 15

The 88mm Artillery Gun

On the morning of 21 November 1944, a total of 1,291 bomber aircraft of the USAAF had taken off from their bases in England, made their way across the English Channel, and continued their journey over Nazi-occupied Europe, en route to attack a large chemical complex deep in the heartland of Germany, at Leuna. By the time the raid was over, 567 of the American aircraft had been damaged and a further 25 had been lost, either shot down by German anti-aircraft guns, German fighter aircraft or by collision. By this time in the war the once mighty Luftwaffe was a shadow of its former self, but German anti-aircraft units were still holding their own in some areas of the country. Their cause had been greatly helped by the addition of 88mm Flak guns and even larger weapons to their defensive arsenal.

One of the American aircraft that took part in the raid that day was a B-17 Flying Fortress from the United States Eighth Air Force, stationed at RAF Molesworth in Cambridgeshire. Its pilot was Werner George Goering who, not surprisingly, acquired himself the nickname of 'Kraut'.

By the time of the raid on Leuna, Goering had already flown a full combat tour of thirty-five missions, so had the right to go home or become an instructor. Instead, he volunteered to fly a second combat tour, and completed a further fourteen missions before the end of the war.

Having dropped their bombs Goering and his crew turned and made for home. His co-pilot that day, as usual was Second Lieutenant Jack P. Rencher. But it had been a far from uneventful raid, and their aircraft had sustained a number of hits from the German 88mm anti-aircraft flak guns. It was touch and go as to whether Goering would make it back to his base. The damage caused by the German Flak guns had resulted in the loss of his two port engines, which Goering had to shut down after they began smoking, whilst revving up his two remaining engines so that he could keep his aircraft in the air. During the raid a German shell had passed right through the cockpit from underneath the aircraft, between Goering and Rencher, without exploding. Goering was unscathed whilst Rencher suffered a concussion and temporary deafness.

By the time Goering made it to the English Channel, he was already struggling to maintain height. He made land on England's south coast, before turning his aircraft towards his home base. As they approached Molesworth Goering's B-17 Flying Fortress had already begun to stall, and it took all his skills as a pilot to prevent it from crashing into the ground. He was losing power, was extremely low on fuel and the aircraft had begun violently vibrating. Goering crash landed in a field adjacent to the main runway, but the aircraft landed on its belly and eventually skidded to standstill. Goering and all of his crew were alive and well, if not a little shaken by their endeavours. Their aircraft resembled a wreck, and it was hard to believe that Goering had managed to keep it in the air long enough to make it back to Molesworth.

The German anti-aircraft Flak guns had certainly done their job as best they could, as Goering's aircraft had a total of 245, bullet, shell and Flak holes throughout its fuselage. How none of the crew had been wounded or killed was a miracle.

Goering, born in Salt Lake City, Utah, in the United States on 11 March 1924, had enlisted in the United States Army Air Force in 1942 just after his 18th birthday. His parents, Karl and Adele Goering were both born in Germany, and Karl Goering claimed to be the brother of Hermann Goring, head of Nazi Germany's Luftwaffe. In Stephen Frater's 2012 book, *Hell Above Earth,* it is stated that research which had been conducted in 2010, proved that Karl and Hermann were not in fact related.

The FBI obviously were not absolutely certain of where Werner Goering's true loyalties lay, because they had instructed his co-pilot, Second Lieutenant Jack Rencher to shoot Goering if he attempted to crash land his aircraft or bail out whilst flying over Germany or German-occupied Europe. As for Goering, he survived the war and remained in service after it, transferring to the newly formed United States Air Force in 1947. He finally retired in 1965 having attained the rank of lieutenant colonel. He died in 2012 at the age of 88.

Despite the restrictions placed on Germany at the end of the First World War, by the Treaty of Versailles, especially in a military sense, companies such as Krupp and Rheinmetall, had managed to find ways to continue their research, development and production of such weapons as the 88mm Flak 18 gun, without breaching the terms and conditions of the Treaty. By 1936, with the Nazi Party having been in power for three years, the greatly improved 88mm Flak 18 gun was in full production, which was also a breach of the conditions of the Treaty of Versailles, but as those who were tasked with inspecting such breaches, not knowing of the infringement, the modified version of the 88mm gun was already in the hands of the German Army.

Krupps and Rheinmetall had not just built new models of the 88, they had totally redesigned it. The main improvements included making it semi-automatic. It had a much improved base that made it far more stabilised, which was especially important after it had been fired. The new version allowed for the barrel to be moved a full 360 degrees, greatly improving its effectiveness, and a proficient gun crew was capable of firing off more than twenty rounds a minute.

The downside of the weapon was that each barrel only had a life expectancy of firing 900 rounds, and with gun crews capable of firing off twenty rounds a minute, that meant the barrel would need changing every forty-five minutes under field conditions whilst engaging the enemy. A system was needed to ensure the procedure of changing the barrel was able to be carried out expediently.

Rheinmetall came up with the solution when they started making the inner tubes of the barrels in three pieces rather than one long section. The main part of the barrel which suffered most damage from the weapon's firing was the middle section, so all the gun crews had to do was replace it. This kept maintenance work and servicing of the gun in the field to a minimum, which in turn meant that it would be out of action for a much shorter period. There were, however, problems with this process. The new three-piece barrel needed to be made of steel, which in wartime Germany was both scarce and expensive. The other aspect was that because the new barrels were heavier, the recoil and equilibrator mechanism also needed modifying to allow for this increase in weight. As the war continued the three-piece inner barrel was replaced with a two-piece section, which was a major improvement.

Part of the barrel included what was called a driving band, which helped to force the shell out of the barrel when the gun was fired. Originally these were made of copper, but eventually they were replaced with ones made of iron. There was also a change in the propellant used for the shells, which caused less wear on the barrel. These improvements helped greatly with the life expectancy of the weapon's barrels which eventually allowed for the firing between 6,000 and 10,000 rounds.

Another amazing feature of the 88mm guns is that their crews could get them ready for action in under three minutes, and could 'pack' them away, hook them up to their vehicle and be on the move in under four minutes. This was even more remarkable when taking into consideration that by the end of the war, the crews of the 88s had been reduced to just six men.

Despite Nazi Germany having fought her way across Europe, she still had the time, capacity and desire to improve her equipment, weaponry and ammunition. By 1944, she had nineteen different types of shells for the 88mm gun. This included high-explosive rounds, armour piercing ones and solid projectiles. The rounds fired by the 88s were designed to fragment into some 1,500 pieces and could damage or destroy an enemy aircraft up to 200 yards away from the epicentre of the exploding shell.

The shells German forces used with their flak weapons contained two types of fuses. One was set to detonate when the fired shell had reached a certain height, and the other had a delayed fuse. Ultimately it did not matter which type of fuse was used in a shell, or how or when it exploded, what mattered was that they did. The resulting explosion sent fragments of jagged steel flying through the air at such velocity, that if they made contact with a member of an aircraft's crew, they would slice through them like a hot knife through butter. The fear that men must have experienced whilst flying through a barrage of exploding Flak, can only be guessed at. Every time a flak shell exploded outside their aircraft, it would have shaken violently as the men inside waited to discover their fate, to find out whether or not this was their time to die or be badly wounded.

Besides the fear of uncertainty, the frustration of not being able to respond, other than by dropping their bombs, must have been hard for these men to take. Once they had dropped their 'pay loads' and were on their way home, their mindset would have improved, but having to make their way through a Flak barrage on their way to their target must have been a nightmare. How these young men managed to hold it together mentally and emotionally is hard to imagine. Besides the worry of being wounded or killed by the exploding Flak, there would have been the greater concern of their pay load of bombs being set off whilst still on board the aircraft. The only saving grace is if that had happened, the subsequent explosion would have blown the men and the aircraft into smithereens, and death would have been instant.

Here are some interesting statistics for the first half of 1944. Out of every 1,000 RAF bomber crews who had served on combat operations, for a period of six months, on average 712 of them were either killed or recorded as being missing in action, with a further 175 who were wounded. This means that only 11 per cent of British air crews survived a Flak barrage whilst part of a force involved in an air raid on an enemy target, and still made it back to their home base.

Those airmen who were part of the RAF's Bomber Command usually had to complete thirty flying operations, which were collectively referred to as an 'operational tour', before they were taken off operational duties and posted to serve on Operational Training Units, where they would help to train the future crews. Completing an operational tour would only take somewhere in the region of between three and five months, placing those who achieved such a feat under unbelievable levels of stress and fatigue. An interesting point to note here is that an 'operation' was only counted as such when the aircraft's bombs had been dropped. If a crew returned early from an operation because they had turned back before reaching their target, or because of an issue such as engine trouble, it did not count towards an operational tour. Late on in the war some flights were only classed as half an operation because the target they had been sent to bomb was deemed not to have been so heavily defended by German anti-aircraft batteries.

For airmen from the United States, it became very confusing to understand what exactly was expected from them. 'Missions' is what the Americans called their 'operations'. They started off having to fly twenty-five missions to complete a 'tour', but that was subsequently raised to thirty missions, before finally ending up having to fly thirty-five. Each extra flight they had to make, was tempting fate, but they had no choice in the matter. They had to fly their aircraft through the German Flak barrages and simply hope that they were going to make it home in one piece.

The 88mm Flak gun alone was credited in 1944 with destroying 6,400 British and American aircraft and damaging a further 27,000. Those are staggering figures, especially when taking in to account that Germany was just months away from losing the war. When the war had finally come to an end, the 88mm Flak gun, was universally determined to have been the best type of gun of the entire war, something that was agreed by all sides. It was hated and feared by Allied airmen, infantry soldiers and tank crews in equal amounts. It truly was an awesomely, frightening weapon. It acquired the somewhat humorous title of being 'anti-everything'.

The beginning of the 88s can be traced back to the First World War and the latter part of 1916. By then it had already been in existence for some years, but as an established weapon with the Imperial German Navy. The German Army adopted it for use on land, and the rest as they say, is history. Not too much work was needed for its 'makeover' as the barrels were already produced by Krupp's and Rheinmetall.

The answer to the question as to how the German navy, or Kriegsmarine, had settled on 88mm as the size of each of the rounds to be fired from the weapon, was simple. An 88mm round weighed approximately thirty-four pounds, and was considered to be the heaviest that an average size man could comfortably carry, without the likelihood of not being able to pick it up or dropping it.

The early models of the German Army's 88mm guns fired a 9.6 kilogramme high explosive shell, which could reach a maximum height of 6,850 metres over a distance of 10,800 metres, which is further than six miles.

Nearly all of Germany's vehicles were drawn by horses during the First World War, although because of its size and weight, the 88mm was usually pulled by a tractor whilst placed on a normal wooden backed trailer of the day. When in its firing position it was stabilised with metal arms which folded out from either side. During the Second World War, the 88 was usually towed by a Sd.Kfz 7 or a Sd.Kfz 11 half-track vehicle, which had enough seats to cater for the weapon's ten-man crew, and it was also big enough to carry a sufficient amount of ammunition.

In Closing

The $64,000 question that needs answering is, were anti-aircraft defences, such as Flak guns, barrage balloons, searchlight units and fighter aircraft, an effective form of defence? Although this book is specifically about German air defences, the same question it is also relevant to the other sides involved in the Second World War. Personally, I believe they did have a useful defensive purpose for any nation. The first relevant point to mention is the fear factor. For any Allied air crew sent on an air raid to somewhere in German-occupied Europe, knowing they were going to have to fly through a barrage of Flak to get to their intended target and drop their payload of bombs, could not have been a pleasant experience.

If the German anti-aircraft batteries continuously fired their guns skywards, they would form a 'blanket' of Flak explosions, which eventually the Allied aircraft would have to fly into if they were to drop their bombs on their intended target, so the more aircraft that were involved in the raid, then the more likelihood there was of the German anti-aircraft units recording a hit.

Another tactic which had value and purpose was the combination of barrage balloons, set thousands of feet up in the sky, which in turn forced the Allied bombers to fly at a higher altitude. In some cases this would have been above the cloud level, making it problematical for them to identify their target and then jettison their payload of bombs. Add to this German fighter aircraft attacking the Allied bombers from above, and the potential for inflicting heavy losses on them was greatly increased.

Were anti-aircraft batteries ever going to prevent air raids from taking place? No, they were not, nor were they going to prevent the damage and death that was the result of such raids. But despite already knowing this, the German authorities had to be seen to be doing something to try to protect their people from the death and destruction that the Allied air raids brought with them, after all, the Nazis had promised so much to their people, and if they couldn't protect them in their own homes, keeping them 'on board' for the rest of the war, however long that might be, was always going to be difficult.

About the Author

Stephen is a retired Police officer having served with Essex Police as a constable for thirty years between 1983 and 2013. His sons, Luke and Ross, were members of the armed forces, collectively serving five tours of Afghanistan between 2008 and 2013. Both were injured on their first tour. This led to Stephen's first book *Two Sons in a Warzone – Afghanistan: The True Story of a Father's Conflict*, which was published in October 2010.

Both of his grandfathers served in and survived the First World War, one with the Royal Irish Rifles, the other in the Merchant Navy, whilst his father served in the Royal Army Ordnance Corps during the Second World War.

Stephen corroborated with one of his writing partners, Ken Porter, on a book published in August 2012, *German POW Camp 266: Langdon Hills*. Steve and Ken collaborated on a further four books in the Towns and Cities in the Great War series by Pen & Sword. Stephen has also written other titles in the same series of books, and in February 2017 his book, *The Surrender of Singapore: Three Years of Hell 1942-45*, was published. This was followed in March 2018 by *Against All Odds: Walter Tull, the Black Lieutenant*, and in January 2019, *A History of the Royal Hospital Chelsea,*

1682-2017: The Warrior's Repose, which he wrote with his wife, Tanya. In 2018 saw the publication of *Animals in the Great War*. In 2019 his book on Britain's worst maritime disaster, *The Lancastria Tragedy*, was published. His latest books include *Stalag 383 Bavaria*, a history of the WWII camp, the escapees and the liberation, and *The Air Transport Auxiliary at War*.

March 2019 saw the publication of his book *Disaster before D-Day: Unravelling the Tragedy of Slapton Sands*. In March 2020, his book on *Mystery of Missing Flight F-BELV*, incorporated the personal story of the death of his uncle during the Vietnam war. The same month saw the publication of *City of London at War 1938-45*. April 2020 saw the publication of *Holocaust: The Nazis' Wartime Jewish Atrocities* and in June 2020, his book entitled, *Churchill's Flawed Decisions: Errors in Office of the Greatest Britain*.

Stephen has also co-written three crime thrillers which were published between 2010 and 2012, which centre round a fictional detective, named Terry Danvers.

When not writing, Tanya and Stephen enjoy the simplicity of walking their four German Shepherd dogs early each morning, at a time when most sensible people are still fast asleep in their beds.

Sources

www.lonesentry.com
www.wikipedia.com
www.thirdreichruins.com
www.ww2db.com
www.lincsaviation.co.uk
www.forces.net
www.forces-war-records.co.uk
www.bbc.co.uk
www.historynet.com
www.erenow.net
Hell Above Earth. Stephen Frater 2012

Index

Allied Combined Bomber
Offensive, 72
Altenmarkt, 142

Barrage Balloons, 84, 85, 86,
87, 88, 189
Bensusan-Butt, David, 15
Bergrheinfeld, 70
Blackett, Professor, 19
Bochum, 150, 152
Bohlen, 138
Bomber Command, 18, 19,
20, 27, 28, 90, 92, 138,
150, 152, 167, 169, 175,
185
Braunschweig, 169
Bruneval, 103, 104, 105,
106, 107
Brunswick, 132, 133, 137
Butt Report, 15, 16, 17, 18

Chaff, 89
Charlottenburg, 30
Chemnitz, 138
Cherwell, Lord, 19

'Dehousing paper', 19
Deutsche Star GmbH
Company, 66
Dornier, 217, 139, 172
Dortmund, 150, 152, 153
Dresden, 138, 153, 173, 174,
175, 177
Duisburg, 149, 150, 168
Dusseldorf, 152

Essen, 152

Fichtel & Sachs Factory, 66
Flak Corps, 4, 42, 43
Flak Corps I, 2
Flak Corps II, 2
Flak Corps III,
Flak Corps IV, 3
Flakgruppen, 1
Flakkorps, 1
Flak Guns, 76, 78, 80, 82,
180, 181, 182, 187, 188,
189
Flak 18, 10, 13
Flak 30, 11, 48

Flak 36, 10
Flak 37, 10
Flak 40, 8, 9, 12, 13
Flak 43, 9, 10
Flakscheinwerfer, 79, 81
Flak, Heavy, 116, 117
Flak, Light, 47, 49, 50, 116,
    117, 151
Flak towers, 6, 76, 143
Flakturm I, 8
Flakturm II, 9
Flakturm III, 9
Flakturm IV, 9
Flakturm V, 9
Flakturm VI, 9
Flakturm VII, 9
Flakturm VIII, 9
Flakvierling 38, 10, 75
Flakzwilling, 13
Fliegerabwehrkanone, 59,
    115
Flugzeugabwehrkanone, 4
Flying Fortresses, B-17, 60, 61,
    62, 63, 64, 65, 67, 70, 90,
    154, 170, 179
Focke-Wulf Fw 190, 62, 172
Frankfurt, 153
Freya Radar System, 89, 91

Gebirgsflak 30, 10
Gebirgsflak 38, 9, 11
German 88mm Gun, 4, 5, 42,
    44, 69, 75

German Air Defences, 109, 111,
    112, 119, 123, 127, 130, 133,
    134, 135, 142, 148, 149, 155,
    157, 160, 162, 164, 167
German Air Force Flak
    Artillery, 41, 51
German Air Ministry, 121
German Electric Company, 77
German Flak, 115, 136
German Girls, League of, 40
German Maidens, Band of, 40
German News Agency, 166,
    170
Gochsheim, 70
Goering, Werner George, 179,
    180, 181
Gotha, 169

Halbertstadt, 133
Hamburg, 153
Harris, Sir Arthur Travers
    'Bomber,' 20, 22, 70, 139,
    145, 146, 176, 177
Heeresflak, 51
Heinkel He 112, 11, 172
Hitler Youth, 40

Junkers 88, 139, 172

Kommandogerat, 45
Krosigk, Count Schwerin von,
    155
Krupps factory, 149, 182, 187

Kugelfischer, 70
Kugelfischer-George-Schafer
    Factory, 66

Lead tower, 8
Lindemann, Professor
    Frederick, 20
Leitturm, 8, 9

Magdeburg, 132, 138
Mannheim, 49
Messerschmitt Bf 109, 24, 62,
    65, 139, 172, 173
Milch, General Erhard, 162,
    163, 164
Military Intelligence Service
    Bulletin, United States,
    42, 51, 87
Muhlenau und Industrie AG,
    132
Munich, 153

Niederwerrn, 70

Operation Biting, 96, 97, 100
Oschersleben, 133

PaK 40, 12
Panzer IV, 76
Photographic Reconnaissance
    Unit, 93
Pidsley, Reginald, 30
Pointblank, Operation, 72, 73

Portal, Sir Charles, 18

Reichstag, 13
Regensburg, 58, 61, 62, 65
Reinickendorf, 32
Rheinmetall, 182, 183, 187
Rosenheim, 142
Rositz, 138

Schoneberg, 30
Schweinfurt, 58, 59, 62, 63, 64,
    65, 67, 68, 69, 70, 71, 72,
    169
Searchlight, Flak, 77, 78, 79,
    80, 81, 82, 83
Spandua, 30
Stuttgart, 170

Thomas, Wynford Vaughan, 29
Thunderbolt, P-47, 60, 62, 170
Tiergarten, 8, 30, 143

Vereinigte Kugellagerfabriken
    AG Company, the, 66
Voss Strasse, 25, 26

War Department Publication,
    United States, 78
Wilhelmshaven, 22
Wilhelmstrasse, 25, 26
Wuppertal, 152
Wurzburg radar, 45, 91, 95,
    101, 102, 103, 106